Ailsa Fabian was born in Melbourne, where her mother, with two sisters, had built up a thriving fashion business in the years after World War One. Ailsa assumed that, like them, work outside the home would always be central to her life. She lectured in history at Melbourne University before studying sociology at Columbia University, New York, and, after moving to London in 1952, worked in social research and in the fashion business. Then, following marriage to the sculptor Erwin Fabian and the birth of her daughter, she became so entranced by the miracle of Sarah's unfolding engagement with the world, that she chose to be an-almost-full-time mother.

When Sarah died in 1964 while on a family visit to Australia, Ailsa turned to writing. She had published various sociological studies, but *The Daniel Diary*, which records the reactions of her three-year-old son to his sister's death, was her first literary work. It was followed by *The Sarah Journals*.

AILSA FABIAN

A *Shining* *Space*

A Daughter's Life

Matador
9 Priory Business Park
Kibworth Beauchamp
Leicestershire LE8 0RX, UK
Tel: (+44) 116 279 2299
Fax: (+44) 116 279 2277
Email: books@troubador.co.uk
Web: www.troubador.co.uk/matador

SB ISBN 978-1783062-447

British Library Cataloguing in Publication Data.
A catalogue record for this book is available from the British Library.

Typeset in 12pt Adobe Garamond Pro by Troubador Publishing Ltd, Leicester, UK
Printed and bound in the UK by TJ International, Padstow, Cornwall

For Erwin and Daniel,
and my grandchildren Hannah and Zac,
and in memory of Dr Joseph Adler

Take your delight in momentariness,
Walk between dark and dark, a shining space,
With the grave's narrowness...
Robert Graves

'Behold what a marvellous creature lived upon this earth!'
This is the cry to which all biography seeks
to move the world.
Thomas Mann

Her fate to know, in ideal form, a child's life, with
its dependency and limitations, its eager reaching
out for the future, and its fullness of love received
and given. To love, in Michael Balint's wonderful
phrase, 'innocently, unconditionally, as only children
can love.' To love with an adult strength of passion,
and at the end of five years, to die.
The Sarah Journals

Foreword

Sarah Eugenie Fabian, my daughter, died suddenly, on June 22 1964, at the of five, from a bronchial infection. I started almost at once to write about her, in the hope that something of the miracle of love and life that she had been for me and for her father, Erwin, could be saved from oblivion and shared with others. This book is based on the memories I recorded in the first years after her death, when the essence of her vibrant self, and of my love for her, and many details of our life together were still vividly present to me.

When I began, many years ago, very few personal accounts of parenthood and early childhood had been published. That is certainly no longer the case. Academic research into those earliest years has also expanded enormously. In the light of recent reading and thinking, I have asked myself new questions about Sarah, become aware of mysteries that I did not then see or understand, and acquired a more critical attitude to my own behaviour and theories. And through living close to two grandchildren, I have seen that diametrically opposed ways of behaving towards children can have equally happy consequences. I have included some later reflections but nothing has caused me to change what I first wrote about Sarah and our life with her. It remains the vision I had when she was alive.

Contents

I

Before

The cabin was dark and silent as we flew over the Pacific, but I could not sleep. As dawn approached, I looked out over a vast cloud-landscape of deep chasms and craggy summits, tinged pink and apricot and saffron, changing to dazzling white as the light grew stronger. Somewhere, in this beautiful nowhere, I 'decided to have a baby.'

I was between two worlds, on my way home to London after visiting my family in Melbourne, leaving behind me also a brief, impossible love affair, which had ended in the euphoria of mutual renunciation. It was a time for change. Sated with the emotions of grand opera, I considered myself ready to accept the banalities of domestic comedy. Insofar as I imagined it at all, having a baby seemed a very banal thing to do.

I was thirty-five, late enough if I ever wanted children. And in a mild way no doubt I did, although previously the possibility had scarcely been part of my plans, dreams, yearnings or fantasies. I knew nothing about babies, had never felt the slightest interest in them, had hardly ever even held one. When my sister and brother, and friends of my own age, had been producing children, I was on the other side of the world, studying and working. I had thought of myself, at least since my appointment to a university teaching job, as a career academic, primarily and unshakably devoted to learning, and had scoffed at the notion that I would ever abandon research, teaching and writing for marriage and parenthood. But I was also a child of prosperity, who assumed that eventually all the good things of life would come her way. These, it seemed to be generally considered, included children.

I meditated during the flight on my habit of falling in love with gifted, egotistical, dominating men, who dazzled me with visions of myself and my future, based on nothing but their own fantasies. Flattering and exhilarating but not, I now saw, a good foundation on which to build a life of my own. Erwin, with whom I had lived happily for several years, and who was to become Sarah's father, is certainly no flatterer, and that seemed a positive quality.

Back in London, Erwin was not enthusiastic about the proposal that we have a baby, but he neither refused outright nor made any serious attempt to dissuade me. We hardly discussed it. I can't recall any talk about how we would support or care for a child, or how our lives might change. I do remember one occasion when, walking home one night through deserted streets, he said, 'You don't really want a baby, do you?' and instead of argument, mimicked a baby's desolate frantic crescendo of wailing. It was at least an evocation of the future, whereas I merely laughed indulgently.

I took for granted that we would both continue to work, and it didn't enter my head that this might be difficult. My mother had always worked, but I failed to remind myself that she had employed a nurse, a cook and a housemaid. By contrast, neither of us was solidly established in our chosen profession. Erwin worked as a freelance graphic designer. I had taught history at Melbourne University for several years, and then studied sociology at Columbia University in New York, before moving to London. I had done various pieces of social research, but had recently turned down several job offers, to make time for independent study and writing. So I was unemployed. But I must have assumed, without making calculations, that we had enough money. It was family money, derived from the successful fashion business founded and run by my mother and her two sisters, Aunt Nell and Aunt Mary. I had grown up in a matriarchy, in which the women earned more than their husbands, and made all the important decisions, and I seem to have inherited an assumption that I should, and could, pay my own way.

Although we hardly thought about the practical and financial aspects of having a baby, another omission seems to me now even more surprising. We never for a single moment contemplated the awesome truth that we were summoning into existence not just a baby, but a human being with a lifetime before her, who would be our responsibility for many years to come, and whom we would love until the end of our lives. Nor did I reflect that we would be founding a family. I still held the adolescent conviction that family life is boring and constricting.

When I recalled this time, writing about it years later, I was astonished that I could have made and sustained a resolve so momentous with so little thought or longing. I write 'I', not 'we'. Erwin shared responsibility for the baby, but responsibility for what I write is mine. I have not interrogated his past, only my own. I scanned my distant self for any hint of a positive expectation. All I found was one almost-forgotten enthusiasm. Years earlier, I had read books by experimental educationists of the twenties and thirties, and been very moved by their vision of a new openness and equality between children and adults, by Susan Isaacs helping three-year-olds to dissect a dead pet rabbit, and by Marie Paneth staunchly withstanding a sexual inquisition from a bunch of aggressive slum kids. The courage of these women and the radical newness of their vision perhaps gave me a first intimation of the parent I wanted to be.

All parents hope to recreate the childhood which they themselves enjoyed, and at the same time to transform it utterly, so as to bestow on their children everything that had been denied to them. For me, the desire for renewal was always the stronger. I longed to give Sarah, and then her brother, Daniel, what I had missed – not material things, but freely expressed love and shared understanding. My parents certainly loved their children (I was the eldest of three, with a younger sister, Betty, and a brother, Bruce), but they seldom expressed their love either verbally or physically. Nor did they talk to us. I don't recall any teaching about the world, or about morals or manners. Since they both worked, and we were looked after by a succession of nurses, we did not spend much time with them. My most magical memories of childhood are of the wild ocean beaches of Bass Strait, during our summer holidays at Portsea – accompanied by a nurse. It was not an unhappy childhood, but a low-key one.

While I lived with Sarah and Daniel, the belief grew constantly stronger that the past does not impose an iron destiny. There are times when everything can be made miraculously new, and the years of early parenthood are such a time. But when I decided to have a baby these beliefs and longings remained unrecognised.

I have talked of 'decision' for want of a better word, although it is a decision whose fulfilment is beyond our control. And the impulse which beckoned her into the world was too frivolous and lacking in density to be called a decision. More like a whim, a 'mere whim', except that it lasted. Having decided, if that is what I had done, I waited hopefully for more than a year before I became pregnant, but then had an early miscarriage. I was mildly surprised but not particularly distressed. Erwin and I got married as planned – in the fifties it did not occur to us to have a baby without – and felt unexpectedly happier. Another year passed while I continued with the ordinary business of living, unobsessed, brushing aside suggestions that I consult a doctor about why I didn't conceive. It would happen if fate decreed.

When finally I became pregnant with Sarah, I knew at once. Only two weeks before, my last period had begun with an unprecedently copious gush of blood which had already seemed like an annunciation. I visited Dr Adler – Dr Joseph Adler, a charismatic and eccentric physician in private practice, totally dedicated to medicine and to his patients. I had been lucky enough to get to know him several years earlier. He was immediately convinced too, despite an initial negative report from the laboratory. 'I sent them two samples. They must have muddled them; I don't think the other woman is pregnant.' The sense of portent and the mutual certainty still please me, as if they were announcing a miraculous advent.

I received the confirmation that I was pregnant with an upsurge of jubilant sexually-assertive triumph, changed into someone more powerful, fortunate and competent than my usual self. Grown-up at last, I suppose. But it didn't last. A week or two later, I suddenly plummeted into depression. I saw that I had condemned myself to a gloomy imprisonment; I was wilfully throwing away career, energy, beauty and every familiar pleasure of life, from getting up late in the morning (though I don't seem to have worried about sleepless nights), to a future rich in unpredictable opportunities. I didn't exactly regret being pregnant, but I began at last to glimpse that there would be losses too. Even then, I didn't begin to assess them realistically. 'I feel a nightmarish paralysing horror!' was the sort of phrase I used in attempting to exorcise panic through writing. And it did fade, though in the coming months, I often surveyed the future glumly.

But when, soon afterwards, we went on holiday, the shared secret seemed to shine between us with a joyful promise. I felt opulently content. In Venice, instead of accompanying Erwin to the Accademia as soon as it opened in the morning, I sat in a quiet café beside the Grand Canal, reading, or contemplating the dancing reflections of sunlight on water. When I gave birth to a girl, I briefly considered calling her Venetia, after those serene mornings.

We returned home, and I discussed arrangements for the confinement with Dr Adler. He considered whether I should have the baby on the National Health and recommended against; better to put one's trust in a known individual than in a large impersonal organisation. The individual would be a consultant obstetrician if it seemed advisable when the time came. He visited the chosen specialist with me, but did not definitely engage him. If all went well, Dr Adler would deliver the baby himself, 'though I don't take many maternity cases these days. They disrupt all my other work, and I'm getting too old for sleepless nights.' I booked into the private clinic he recommended.

I don't want to justify this reasoning. A few years later, such a programme would have been financially impossible for us. It was possible for us then partly because. Dr Adler, like Erwin and his mother, was a Jewish refugee from Nazism; a sense of shared culture and experience, and an atmosphere of family-like affection and loyalty were perhaps behind his readiness to make an exception for us.

Dr Adler was a follower of the French natural childbirth pioneer Dr Ferdinand Lamaze, whose Paris clinic he had visited, bringing back two wall charts, which he now unfurled for me. One showed stages in the growth of the foetus, the other the physiology of birth. My ignorance of all this had been profound. We were still in an era, although at its very end, when the only labour a woman knew anything about was her own. Coming from a reticent home, living in big cities, self-exiled while relatives and friends had their babies, I hadn't even had the questionable initiation provided by gossip or folklore. My image of childbirth was based on a few scenes from fiction – hushed voices, demands for boiling water (whatever for?), agonized shrieks, and Anna Karenina lying against the pillows convinced that she was dying. Dr Adler's charts banished this murky melodrama before it could make me apprehensive. The clear black outline drawings of the uterus during childbirth had a reassuring logic. First one set of muscles contracts to pull open the cervix. While this is happening you wait passively, and try to minimize pain by relaxing. Dr Adler gave a comical demonstration of the short panting breaths taught by Lamaze. Then, when the cervix is wide open, you must summon strength and courage to push the baby out into the world. It all seemed straightforward, comprehensible, and unfrightening.

The doctor rolled up his charts, and neither of us returned to the subject again. He did not suggest that I join an exercise class, and dismissed the notion of training in relaxation. 'It's not much use teaching women to relax when nothing is happening; they forget it all under stress.' It was an attitude that suited my preference for going it alone. During succeeding visits, he was brisk, rational and humorous, like someone introducing a colleague to an aspect of their common profession which she hasn't previously encountered.

Few books about childbirth had as yet been published. I read what I could find. The obvious first purchase was Grantly Dick-Read's *Childbirth Without Fear*, interesting and reassuring, but written with the condescending praise for his patients that a rider might feel for his horse. How lucky I was to meet with Dr Adler's egalitarianism! A friend lent me a book for prospective mothers which contained a horrendous description of the prolonged confinement of a seventeenth-century French aristocrat, attended by a midwife the sign of whose profession was a long pointed fingernail for piercing the membrane. Well that was long ago! I got my copy of the essential handbook of the time, Dr Spock's *Baby and Child Care*, whose advice begins only when there is a baby to care for. In the Public Library, I found Sarah Campion's *National Baby*, about having a baby on the National Health, from which I retain a picture of the author spending the last weeks of pregnancy in an attic, typing frantically to finish a book, and nourishing herself on Bemax and bananas. It was the only personal account I came across. Today's ubiquitous public discussion of maternity and baby care, illustrated with countless personal stories, did not get under way until fifteen or so years later, ten years after I started to write this book.

I accepted the scarcity of information as belonging to the natural order of things. Nor do I regret it now. It meant that the reality of giving birth, and of a sudden new presence on earth, came to me with a fierce impact not diffused or mediated by the experience of others.

But I thought astonishingly little about what was in store for me, or about the coming baby, as I found when I reread my diary – a rambling meditation which I was in the habit of keeping at times of dissatisfaction with myself and my life. I see that I remained preoccupied with stubborn personal failings, familiar from both earlier and later years. The few references to the baby are brief, egocentric and foreboding: 'I will become stupid, useless and without opportunities. . . no longer be myself. . . deprived of beauty and energy and career. . . barely notice in myself any pleasure in the promise of that baby. . .' I never ask what I might do to minimise these disasters. Then, at about four months, the diary suddenly breaks off, not to be recommenced during Sarah's lifetime.

Meanwhile I made minimal preparations for her arrival. With some curiosity but no daydreaming, I bought the items listed by the hospital, including piles of nappies ('nursery squares'), both gauze and towelling. I felt thankful that most of the essential clothing arrived, without effort on my part, from my family in Australia. But I transformed the stacks of nappies into decorative objects by tying them up in bundles with turquoise tape, and bound the new cot blankets with ribbon, the white one in blue and the blue in royal purple. I bought a pale blue lacquered-wicker bassinet on wheels because it looked attractive and sturdy, though I didn't picture a baby in it. No book had reminded me that a cradle should rock, and I discovered only later that I could push the bassinet to and fro to lull a fretful infant to sleep. It became one of the foundations of Sarah's happiness, and then of Daniel's, and cradled three more babies before disappearing from sight in the underground flow of baby-goods from old to new mothers.

As the months passed, I sank into narcissistic content. Every afternoon I fell asleep on the sofa. At parties I sat in matronly isolation, unashamed and unenvious, with nothing to say. I rather enjoyed feeling clumsy and helpless, and attracting a solicitude from Erwin which previously I had neither wanted nor been given. Even in the last physically awkward weeks, I wasn't impatient, but savoured the final moments of irresponsibility, like a traveller glad to remain comfortably seated until the plane has taxied to a stop, before she must plunge into the steamy confusion of a new country.

II

Birth

On a rainy Saturday morning, the second of May 1959, Erwin drove me to the nursing-home by appointment, Dr Adler and the consultant having decided that as I was an 'elderly primipara', labour should be induced early. The nursing-home, in a quiet street in Marylebone, looked like a well-to-do private house. A maid in cap and apron showed us into a Persian-carpeted hall with a mahogany table for mail. My room, admittedly the cheapest, looked more like that of a modest boarding house. It had a flimsy wardrobe, a cheap dressing-table and a faded chintz armchair; only the hospital bed recalled the clinic. The maid brought us tea and biscuits, and then Erwin was politely asked to leave. Despite Adler's progressive views, no-one suggested that Erwin might be present at the birth of his child.

I passed the rest of the day in a curious limbo. The room gave onto a light-well and was rather dark; the faint sound of a radio came up from the basement, but otherwise there was no sign of life, either from within the building or from outside. Eventually two young nurses appeared and escorted me along corridors and up and down stairs to a homely bathroom, where they scrubbed my back for me and towelled me dry. It was like finding myself in the nursery wing of a country house, in the charge of two deferential but firm nannies. They returned me to my room and gave me the first of the labour-inducing injections.

In the middle of the afternoon the rain began again. I sat in the armchair in my dressing-gown, reading, mildly bored, experiencing no unwonted sensations and having little curiosity about what would happen next. When eventually something did happen it was so undramatic that I remember now only the runic utterance, 'You'd better get into bed. You won't be going home now the waters have broken.' I sat up in bed, eating bread-and-butter and iced sponge cake, while a nurse unpacked my suitcase, tossing the turquoise tapes from the bundles of nappies into the waste basket (whence I later retrieved them), and arranging the baby-clothes tidily in dressing-table drawers. She kept out a set of clothes and some nappies, then fetched a bassinet, which she made up snugly, putting a hot-water bottle between the sheets. I watched these activities with astonishment. No baby was to be seen; the room held no tension of expectancy and I didn't feel the slightest awareness that within my body a living creature, almost a human being, was ready to enter the world. 'But there isn't a baby here!' I said. 'There will be,' the nurse replied matter-of-factly. I didn't feel convinced.

Somewhat later I started to feel little stabs of pain in my back and belly, which gradually became stronger. By the time Erwin called in at about nine o'clock, they were absorbing most of my attention, and I greeted him very perfunctorily. After he had left I was settled down for the night with a cup of Ovaltine and a straightening of the bedclothes. I asked the night-nurse to look in from time to time, though I had already discovered that the bell was answered promptly.

I closed my book, turned out the light, and in the darkness submitted to the recurring pains, which gradually increased in intensity, until bodily sensations began to assume hallucinatory shapes, and the slightest sound to seem an intolerable drain on energy. Just ordinary pain though, no worse than a familiar menstrual pain, endured simply because it was there, not as a sign of the immanence of a new life.

Soon after midnight, Dr Adler arrived, prepared to stay the night, and settled down in the armchair to try to get some sleep. In the small hours, he bent over me with a concerned expression on his face, urging me to take the short panting breaths that were taught in the Paris clinic, demonstrating them once more, assuring me that they would ease the pain. But they were just another exasperating intrusion, like noise, and I found it more soothing to take deep gulps of air and exhale very slowly, pushing the pain away with my breath. He tried rubbing my back and that too seemed unbearably irritating. Dr Adler, a self-effacing observer, who respected the autonomy of the individual, accepted at once that I was the best judge of what helped me, and didn't ask me to give his palliatives another try.

Once, left alone, I got out of bed to pee, and found that I couldn't, and couldn't climb back either. And I remember in the grey early morning the doctor asking irritably for the breakfast he had been promised, and finally going out to look for it. I could smell the rain-washed freshness of the Sunday streets. Later, a nurse offered me a whiff of gas and I gulped it greedily, not consciously abandoning the resolution taken months earlier to meet the birth challenge in full awareness but forgetting why I was there, and understanding only that the mask would bring merciful ease. Dr. Adler did not snatch it away or order me to relinquish it, but asked gently if I could do without. I could and did.

A long time went by, more than twelve hours since Erwin's visit, blank now except for those few remembered moments. I was asked if I felt a need to 'bear down', and, too delirious to know what was meant, but eager for release, I nodded. There was a little flurry of activity, but it subsided when a nurse, probing between my legs, announced that it was too soon. I lay back and submitted again to the necessity for mere endurance.

Suddenly the atmosphere changed. People crowded into the room. They whisked away the bedclothes and draped clean sheets over my belly and legs. I sat up and watched Dr Adler scrub his hands and direct the opening of a shiny biscuit-tin from John Bell and Croyden, which disgorged a quantity of packets wrapped in white paper. Selecting from among them, a nurse helped the doctor to put on a green cotton overall, cap, mask and rubber gloves. Meanwhile another nurse cleared books and clutter from the bedside table. When I protested at losing the little green leather travelling clock my mother had given me, she put it on a high shelf where I could see it. The time was exactly midday.

I was no longer stupefied and isolated by pain. The occasion still had no purpose beyond itself, but it had turned into a performance in which I had a leading role. I felt suddenly alert and confident, buoyed up by a sense of authority. A nurse stood at each side of the bed and supported my legs whenever a contraction signalled the need to push. I pushed mightily. Soon I was sweating heavily, and stripped off my bed-jacket. The nurses could see when a contraction was beginning and called encouragement, but I could feel it even earlier, and presently it was I who gave the word for them to lift and hold me. The spasms didn't last long. As they ebbed, I sank back and rested in the delicious relief of pain withdrawn.

But I was less conscious of pain during the labour-bouts than of urgent necessity. I was under an absolute imperative to expel from my body a foreign object whose weight I could now feel. Still half-delirious, seeing the figures around me as an imprisoning wall, driven as much by dread as by hope, knowing that the only way out of the ordeal was through my own determination, I pushed. I wasn't struggling to bring a child into the world; there was still no imminent human presence. Only something alien and heavy as stone, which I must force through the taut barrier of flesh.

The end came suddenly and with surprising ease. The doctor bent over me. I felt the weight of his body against my legs, a brief stab of a different pain, a sudden release of tension, and the sensation of something slippery being lifted away from me. Someone called out, 'It's a girl!' and I looked up and saw her, naked and glistening, dangled by her heels. I felt an enormous surge of triumph and relief. 'It won't be as bad next time, will it?' I asked the doctor. He laughed. 'They usually say, "I'm not letting that bastard near me again!"' I looked at my clock and saw that it was twenty past twelve.

'I'll have to put in a stitch. I had to make a little nick because the membrane didn't stretch enough.' I hadn't identified the cause of that last sharp pain, and the stitch didn't really hurt, but the knowledge of that cut remained, to throw a shadow of apprehension over my next confinement. There was some anti-climactic cleaning, clearing-away, straightening of bedclothes and plumping of pillows. Then she was laid beside me, wrapped in a blanket, which revealed only her pearly face and a patch of damp black hair. My life changed in that instant. I recognised the human weight of her existence and knew that I was bound in love to her forever.

She lay there for only a very little while. Dr Adler had rung Erwin and handed me the phone. 'Can you leave her here while I talk to him?' I asked. But they took her away, and I was too jubilant to feel more than fleetingly disappointed, and too tired. 'Would you like some lunch?' someone asked, and I remained sufficiently myself to enquire what there was for lunch, before falling asleep.

Erwin had worked through the night without telling his student assistant that he was about to become a father. Years later we talked about this aloofness from the birth of his first child. 'I rather resented it,' he said, 'but when the doctor rang I felt suddenly its marvellous to have a daughter.' When he came to the hospital in the afternoon, a nurse brought her to the room and he held her in his arms before I did. The scene alternates in my memory with another: in the same room, in the same chair, Erwin holding the baby Sarah, Sarah holding her new-born brother, the baby Daniel, both gazing down with the same tender astonished smile.

No immediate question about going home arose, as it would nowadays. I had been told that I would remain in hospital for a week or more; in fact I stayed there for ten days. I was woken at a quarter to six each morning with a cup of tea, which I drank with intense pleasure while waiting for the baby to be brought. I discovered with surprise that breast-feeding needed to be learned. At first she fumbled and nuzzled ineffectually because my breasts were so swollen with milk that the still nameless baby could not catch hold of my nipple. Then one of the nurses, a young girl with straight fair hair and a nun's dedicated face, cupped her hand behind the baby's head and pushed it forcefully down onto my breast with a circular movement like screwing a knob onto a bedpost. Somehow it worked.

The baby soon established a pattern of feeding which she kept as long as I nursed her. She sought my nipple eagerly as soon as I held her, and sucked steadily and vigorously but only for a short while, much shorter than nurses and baby books, with their emphasis on timing, thought right. Then she stopped abruptly and no coaxing would make her start again. Instead of interpreting this as failure, some beneficent instinct made me proud of her precocious independence and of our self-sufficiency. When she was satisfied, I held her on my knee, savouring the miracle of her existence, and talking quietly to her. She had pale creamy skin, definite features, and fine dark hair, which the nurses brushed into a little cocky-crest. I crooned endearments, calling her my dove, my pigeon, my peacock, weasel, badger, wombat, rose, paeony, daffodil.

From the beginning she reached out actively towards the world. Every time she was with me I noticed new gestures of exploration, so many that on the second day of her life I resolved to keep a diary to record them. I attempted to memorise a growing list to save up until I got back to my typewriter, but it soon became too long to repeat, and by the time I got home the impulse to see her as an object for scientific study had vanished. Now all those impressions are lost. All except one, of her burrowing into my breast with such force and eagerness, like a small determined animal, a squirrel or a possum, that I shook with silent laughter.

Between feeds she remained in the nursery and I did not see her, except for two hours in the morning, when her bassinet was brought to my room. That was the rule of the clinic, and I did not think of challenging it. During pregnancy I had been attracted by enthusiastic accounts of the new 'rooming-in' system, and had regretted in advance that I would miss out on its intimate pleasures, but after her birth these regrets vanished. I luxuriated in quiet and privacy, and didn't even pay much attention to her during those morning hours when she was with me. She slept, which was what she needed, and I read, telephoned, and received visitors. She breathed so lightly and lay so still that when

Cecily de Monchaux came to see me, we talked for ten minutes or so before Cecily realised that the baby was there too, asleep in the wicker basket. A friend since the days when we both taught at Melbourne University, Cecily was both academic psychologist and practising psychoanalyst, and her comments provide a chorus to my tale.

Towards the end of my stay, I was taken down to the nursery when it was empty, during this morning period. I was in this clinic several times and I never saw another baby, or another mother. It was my only complaint. I had just discovered that I lived in a world where babies – or at least a baby – existed, and I would have liked to share impressions. In the nursery I was shown how to bath and dress her, and that was all the instruction in baby-care that I received.

She was born at the beginning of one of those rare English summers when the sun shines continuously. In my memory, the rain stopped streaming down the window ten minutes before her birth, and every afternoon during the first week of her life the sun crept across the light-well and into my room. On the second Sunday I put on my maternity suit, having discovered with surprise that I couldn't yet fit into normal clothes, and Erwin drove us to Regent's Park. Arm in arm we walked slowly round the lake, watching the boating couples and the parading families. Tulips in regimented squares of yellow, white, purple, orange, and scarlet echoed our sense of triumph.

At first the baby remained nameless. We had not discussed names before she was born, and now there seemed no urgency. It was not until several weeks after we took her home, that Erwin went to the Marylebone Registrar's Office to register her birth as Sarah Eugenie. As soon as the name Sarah was suggested, we both accepted it. I didn't think of it as a Jewish name, not knowing then that the Nazis had compelled all Jewish women in Germany to add Sarah to their names. On the contrary, it seemed to have no associations with the contemporary world; I had never known anyone called Sarah, and it evoked strangeness, beauty, rarity; 'Princess', a book from the library gave as its meaning. 'Sarah' seemed a very private choice, and I was surprised to read in The Times a few months later that it had been the most popular girl's name of the year. We debated for a long time over a second name, but once chosen, 'Eugenie' also seemed right. It was the name of Sarah's great-grandmother, Erwin's maternal grandmother, who had been murdered by the Nazis in Theresienstadt.

Despite never having looked after a baby for as much as an hour, I still didn't wonder how I would cope when I took her home. There would be no-one to help or advise. My mother would soon arrive from Australia, but she was too diffident to covet responsibility. My mother-in-law, who lived near to us in London, had never had to acquire competence in practical matters. Alone, I, or we, would have fumbled and dithered, a prey to doubt, confusion and panic. But Dr Adler suggested that I engage a nurse and dutifully, like Levin told that he should buy sweets to celebrate his engagement, I rang the agency he recommended, and fate sent me Jennifer. She was scarcely more than a child herself, pretty, pink-cheeked, and unassuming, but she had worked as a baby-health visitor in the rough world of New Zealand timber camps, and appeared very confident. Wearing a lilac linen dress, she came to the hospital on the tenth morning, and carried Sarah out into the sunshine.

From then on, without waiting for instructions, Jennifer assumed charge of the baby, of me, and of the household, establishing a pattern that filled the days. Feeding, bathing, changing, putting down to sleep succeeded each other, never pedantically timed but veering back towards their appointed hour after each deviation. She brought me breakfast in bed, ordered me back there for a nap after lunch, and tended the wounds of childbirth and nursing; my only duties were to nurse Sarah, and prepare two meals a day for the rest of the household. I was surprised by her tacit assumption of authority, but although I have often resented and rejected advice, I immediately accepted the routine which she seemed, not so much to impose, as to mediate. It seemed the order of Nature herself.

The day now began in the first light of early-summer dawn, soon after 4 a.m., when Jennifer brought the baby to me in bed, clean, changed and hungry. I awoke without reluctance, glad that the nurse responded to the baby's demand and not just to the clock. She left me alone with Sarah, and I lay against the pillows, cradling her close to me while she drew in the tingling flow of milk, and the day slowly brightened over the garden. They were mornings of enchanted contentment.

Then we all slept again. After breakfast, I watched Jennifer bath Sarah in a plastic basin on the bathroom chest-of-drawers. She rested the tiny body on her forearm, cupping the small head with one hand while she soaped her fine black hair and gently rinsed her face with water, before lowering her into the tub. When she was lifted out, the baby lay comfortably across the depth of the chest, although only a few weeks later she would use its full length and it would seem unbelievable that she had been small enough to lie across it.

All Jennifer's movements were deft and precise. I copied them, learning a new technology: to dress Sarah on a chest or a table rather than on my knee; to fold and fasten a nappy in an exact and particular way; to lift her half-naked body casually by the heels when changing her; to provide a bowl of warm water and swabs of cotton-wool for cleaning her bottom; to swathe her firmly in a shawl before laying her on her side to sleep. Imitating Jennifer, I gradually acquired her confidence.

I never felt that she was an intruder between me and Sarah. A few edgy scenes arose out of the difficulties of sharing a small flat, but never any tension over Sarah. Jennifer was too young to intimidate me, and too full of youthful optimism to be jealous. A Good Fairy indeed, although it was only years later, after experience with other nurses, that I fully appreciated our luck. But my rapidly increasing self-assurance had other sources as well. Although at first I left nearly all the work of looking after Sarah to Jennifer, the most important role was always mine. My milk sustained her life and brought her its first intense pleasure. And before that, the essential beginning of confidence was the moment of her birth without the help of drugs or instruments, which left me with an enduring sense of achievement.

III

Summer Idyll

When Sarah was three weeks old, my mother and her sister, Aunt Nell, arrived from Australia to see the new grandchild, an arrival timed with self-effacing diplomacy so as not to break into the intimacy of our first days with the baby. Their journey was also a business trip, the last in a series stretching back to the early twenties. They stayed as usual at the Savoy, telephoned their agent every morning, and visited the autumn collections, but the old urgency and tension had gone. Even Aunt Nell, who had always been more pugnaciously identified with the business than my mother, went the rounds of garment collections and fabric houses as if simply calling on old acquaintances.

They retained, however, their air of independence and self-sufficiency, ordering drinks for us in the Savoy bar with the assurance of women accustomed to paying with their own hard-earned cash. After taking us out to dinner, they insisted that we leave them to walk back to the hotel by themselves. We watched them set off, looking frail in their summer dresses of chiffon and lace, tenderly solicitous of each other, Aunt Nell worried that my mother, who had had an operation for cancer, might get over-tired, and my mother watching out for unevenness in the pavement so that she could warn Aunt Nell, whose eyesight was poor. They were generous with dinner invitations, which, thanks to Jennifer, we were free to accept, but more often they visited us at home. On Sunday afternoon after lunch, sitting in the garden, between the dustbins and a clothesline of nappies, grandmother and great-aunt murmured their appreciation.

My mother was deferential towards me as a mother, accepting of Jennifer's methods, and rather shy with Sarah, asking, when occasionally she was left in charge, for detailed instructions to cover every contingency. She had not arrived bearing gifts but listened for any hint of something I needed, and then insisted on paying for it. We chose a pram together, soberly grey-lined because I had read that light-coloured linings were dazzling for a baby's eyes, and made a special excursion to Oxford Street to equip it with an absurd, fringed sun-canopy.

Our pleasure in Sarah's existence was the first deep emotion my mother and I had been able to share without strain for a very long time, since my almost-forgotten childhood, the time of one isolated memory, of clasping my arms round her neck at bedtime and saying passionately, 'I won't let you go! I'll never let you go!' That unreserved love had disappeared quite early, for reasons I only dimly understand. The rift had been deepened by differences in education, and by the wide gap in values and behaviour between our generations. We hadn't had open rows, but behaved towards each other with a coolness that was cautious and bewildered on her side, self-righteous and resentful on mine. Guilty and contrite too. I had lived in

London because it was a long way from home, and had written to her regularly, in a gesture of reparation that I knew was inadequate. Now, my contentment, and my mother's relief that I had at last achieved the blessings of marriage and motherhood, brought us together in a tacit reconciliation.

Those first weeks at home with Sarah, shared with Jennifer and my mother and Aunt and filled with simple pursuits, were like a convalescence. Convalescing from what? Not the physical strains of pregnancy and labour – ten days in hospital were more than sufficient for that. Convalescence perhaps after years of solitude, lightened by intervals of being in love, but not by much loving.

When my mother and Aunt Nell left for the customary visit to Paris, we said goodbye to Jennifer also. Despite my newly acquired skills, I felt awesomely aware of our fragile isolation, the three of us alone together, separated from help by a barrier of time, distance and ignorance of when help might be needed. But no emergency interrupted the tranquil rhythm of our new lives.

All her life Sarah was a good sleeper. I doubt that I could have survived with equanimity long bouts of fretfulness or continuously interrupted nights, but I was never tested. By the time Jennifer left, Sarah slept until six every morning, and continued to sleep for most of the day. For more than a year, it was only in the afternoon that she was awake for long. I began to wonder if she slept too much, and said so to Cecily, who laughed. 'It's if she didn't sleep that you'd have to worry.'

She continued to nurse easily. I always had enough

milk, and she took what she needed. Did hunger sometimes assail her 'as if she were being torn by wolves', as one psychoanalytic authority put it. If so, it can only have been fleetingly, for I seldom kept her waiting – although one small incident suggests how different things could have been. One hot day I stripped off her woolly jacket before I gave her my breast. She yelled so desperately that it was several minutes before she calmed down enough to suck.

Sarah was at her liveliest after a feed, and we conversed then, in smiles and looks and caresses, and later in those universal first games of nodding and head-shaking and pretend disappearances. From the beginning I talked to her in words too, about herself, and what I was doing, and the things around us. If I had to move away from her, I told her where I was going and why, assuring her I would return soon, and calling while out of sight, so that she would not imagine I had ceased to exist. I believed she could interpret my tone of voice long before she could understand the words.

As the days became warmer and she was awake for longer, the look of vulnerability that seemed to demand the protection of long-sleeved Viyella nighties faded. I made two dresses for her, quintessential baby dresses with gathered skirts, puff sleeves and decorative feather-stitching. They looked delicate, but were made of tough quick-drying non-iron muslin. I felt strongly about her clothes. I wanted them to be pretty but spare, and made the dresses myself because those I could buy seemed to me fussy, or impractical, or shoddy. The one-piece babygro had not yet appeared, nor did I have the stud-fastened cotton jersey nighties printed with flowers or animals that my sister-in-law Ruth later sent from New York. 'I'm making two dresses for Sarah,' I told Aunt Nell, with the pride I felt in everything I did for her. She laughed. 'You'll need more than that. What if she's sick?' But she never was, and for months she seldom wore anything in the daytime but one of my dresses.

I made two dresses for myself also. Last summer's clothes still didn't fit, and there were new requirements of opening down the front and being easy to wash. What pretty prints there were that year! One of my cottons was patterned with blue morning glories, the other with yellow roses. Sarah had a dress printed with yellow roses too, and sometimes we dressed like sisters. As her body became firmer, I carried her tucked under my arm, resting lightly on my hip. When my mother laughed at this casualness, I was pleased. 'But she seems to like it,' she said. I thought that always to cradle her in my arms was to exaggerate her weakness and need for protection. Balanced on my hip, she seemed to move by my side as an equal. Together, in our rose-sprigged dresses, we opened the door to friends who came to pay homage.

Visiting friends, if they had children (most of whom were by now grown-up), always wanted to hold her, and I was surprised by the look of yearning on their faces as they reached out to take her. Not now, when I also rarely hold a baby in my arms.

When they returned from Paris, my mother and Aunt Nell seemed at a loose end, with several weeks to go before their return sailing to Australia. I suggested that we rent a house somewhere in the country for a holiday together. The frantic business trips of the past had never allowed time for holidays. Through friends I found a place on the outskirts of Cambridge, and at my mother's suggestion, to save us housework, the elders booked rooms in a Cambridge hotel. My mother-in-law and Erwin's sister Lilo would also join us for some of the time

We drove to Cambridge, with Sarah asleep on the back seat, and found the house down a narrow lane, its back door unlocked, so that we had only to walk in and take possession. It had three stories, many bedrooms, and downstairs, a drawing room-cum-library and a big kitchen-living room opening onto a secluded overgrown garden. Everything was in a state of extravagant neglect. There were dirty socks hidden in the bedclothes, a stethoscope and a pair of new football boots in the long grass of the garden, and someone's dried-up dinner in the oven. We swept, scrubbed, tidied and summoned repair men, until the house seemed to belong to us, as if we had found it abandoned in the middle of a forest. A cheerful crone whom we had undertaken to employ hobbled in from the garden, accepted the evidence of our labour without comment, charmed us by addressing Sarah as 'Bubba', and disappeared again, never to return.

In Cambridge we got up at six when we heard Sarah's first cry. While the light filtering through to the wide staircase was still grey, we went down to the kitchen, where I sat nursing her at one end of the long table, while Erwin boiled the kettle on the chipped Baby Belling, and made a pot of strong reviving tea. Sarah slept again, and we sat for a long time over breakfast. Then, with the sun streaming through the windows as it did every day that summer, I bathed her in a washing-up basin on the kitchen table, and put her pram, protected by a net, in the wasp-filled garden, before washing a load of nappies and pegging them out on a line near the kitchen door, where Erwin had scythed down a lush growth of nettles. Later in the morning I left Sarah in his charge and drove to the market in Cambridge, to buy tomatoes and greengages and bunches of brilliant dahlias, before picking up the three grandmothers (my mother-in-law also stayed in Cambridge), and returning for a copious lunch.

Afterwards the elders retired to sleep in some of the many spare bedrooms; Erwin painted gouaches of the laden apple-trees and exuberant cabbages in the kitchen garden; I unpegged the stiff-bellied nappies and heaped them on the sofa in the unused drawing-room, before giving myself the pleasure of exploring someone-else's bookshelves. I discovered a family album with photos from the twenties, of figures posed in front of an open touring-car, children riding bicycles and ponies, and families picnicking at the beach; they could have been photos from my own childhood.

As the shadows lengthened, we all met again for tea on the lawn and later drove to the hotel for dinner. Erwin and I crossed the lobby, holding between us the cot in which Sarah was already asleep. It was our first public appearance with her, and we were convinced that everyone who saw her was dazzled by her beauty.

The days passed, until it was time for my mother and

Aunt Nell to return to Australia. We accompanied them to Tilbury and said goodbye at the door of their cabin, where my mother held Sarah for a moment and then gave her back to me without trembling. 'Your mother just loves that baby,' Aunt Nell said.

Back in Cambridge, our days became more varied. Friends came to stay; sometimes we had guests to dinner; in the afternoons we drove out into the country, once tracing the sunken channel of a Roman road across a field of yellow stubble, and picnicking at an ancient crossroads. I walked with Cecily in the evening, talking about books and academic gossip and her new research scheme, elated by a brief escape from domestic preoccupations.

Cecily, drinking her breakfast coffee at the kitchen table while I rinsed Sarah's muslin dress and hung it over the sink to dry, remarked in a surprised tone, 'What a lot of work a baby makes!' I was surprised too, having already accepted the fact that looking after a baby fills the day, so that this agreeable little task didn't seem like work.

Our friend Klaus Friedeberger was taking photographs of Sarah, who was looking rather glum. 'I know how to make her laugh,' I said, and called out to her, 'Pidge, Pidge, Pidge,' using her latest nickname, short for Pigeon, suggested by her warm softly-throbbing body as she rested in my arms after a meal. She smiled winningly, and I was convinced that she appreciated the absurdity of the name, showing that she already had a sense of humour.

We gathered windfall plums and apples in the orchard. Erwin made big bowls of apple puree, and Sarah ate a few spoonfuls, her first solid food. The summer lingered like those of my own remembered childhood. We stayed on until the owners of the house were due to return, and drove down the lane for the last time just as a schoolboy son with a rucksack appeared at the far end.

IV

First Year

We returned to our rented flat, the days shortened, Erwin went to his studio every morning and often didn't return until late at night, and I stayed at home alone with Sarah for most of the day. Not for the entire time, because the house still had that London institution, a resident housekeeper, Mrs Theobald, who lived in two cramped basement rooms divided by the coke furnace, with an outside bathroom. Theo was prepared to keep an eye on Sarah for a few hours, so I wasn't completely fettered, but I used my freedom only for domestic errands, never taking time off to go to an exhibition, or a movie, or even a solitary walk in the park. Although I paid Theo for babysitting, I felt she was doing me a favour, something I was unused to accepting, and I was afraid she would feel imposed on if I stayed out for long. And as yet I didn't feel any twinge of revolt against relentless domesticity.

In the daytime, morning and afternoon, Sarah slept in the garden. So that she wouldn't be bored, I put her pram in a different place each day, always where she could gaze at moving leaves or branches, or, if it rained, in a recess under the balcony from which she could see the sky. I felt proud that she slept out of doors all through the winter.

In her waking hours, I tended and talked to her with rapt absorption, watching as she flaunted new achievements. Her sense of discovery was mine also, a continuous one whose exhilaration I can still recapture, although I remember little of what was discovered. Only that she used to twirl her hands and feet in circles tirelessly, in a way that seemed her own original invention. And to bicycle her legs so energetically that she pulled her white cotton leggings down around her feet and then shook them off, until I learned to tie them round her ankles with the turquoise tapes saved from her bundles of nappies. She lay on a towel on the floor, her white-trousered legs working like rapid pistons, her lips pursed in intense concentration, and her eyes downcast, except when she darted me a quick glance and a triumphant smile.

She showed a lively delight in being the focus of attention. Seated in a circle of friends, or propped on pillows in the bassinet, she would rest her dark eyes on each face in turn, compelling an answering gaze, making sure that no-one's interest strayed, controlling her admirers with instinctive assurance.

She began to eat solid food. I started by steaming vegetables and pushing them through a sieve, but this soon came to seem too much work for the tiny quantity she ate, and like most people I resorted to tins, or, preferably, to glass jars, from which I thought the food would taste better. I warmed her meals in a graceful little steel cream-jug I had bought years before, and fed her with a vermeil coffee spoon from a set we had been given as a wedding present.

Gradually she ceased to be interested in sucking. Psychologists and dictionaries view weaning as a process imposed on a baby from outside. 'Wean, v. To accustom (a child or young animal) to the loss of its mother's milk; to cause to cease to be suckled.' But I didn't cause her to cease to be suckled; she simply ceased to suckle. Noting her obvious indifference, I started to give her milk in a cup, guided by Dr Spock, who thought it 'the most natural of all' if one could cut out an intermediate stage of bottle-feeding. At first she drank very little, and perhaps I felt anxious, because I bought several different plastic training cups, but none made drinking miraculously easy and I soon discarded them as unnecessary gadgets which we could do without, as had countless generations before us.

So I gave her milk in an ordinary cup. Gradually she drank more, and her sucking became very perfunctory, so that, first at one feed and then at another, I stopped putting her to the breast. There doesn't seem to be anything essentially natural about drinking from a cup, but she changed from sucking to sipping as if by some unfolding inner need. I boasted of our achievement to a young doctor I met at a party. 'She'd like a nice soft rubber teat,' he said gloatingly. 'Not as nice as you, I know, but not a bad substitute.'

For a while her appetite seemed to increase inordinately, and I was astonished at the enormous bowls of cereal she ate. Then suddenly, in one of those inexplicable changes that the books don't warn of, and which there seems no point in puzzling over, she would accept only half the amount she had been eating before. Except if Mrs Theobald was feeding her, when she went on obediently opening her mouth as Theo presented spoonful after spoonful.

At Christmas we did not alter our usual celebration for family and friends, and gave her no presents. She was simply there, barefooted and wearing a clean dress and cardigan, propped up in a chair to watch the rest of us open our packages and give her the discarded wrappings to play with. She sat with us for a little while at table, ate a fragment of turkey, and was encouraged by Cecily to gnaw at a gingerbread man until her face and dress were smeared with chocolate. Then she slept, while we ate and drank our way through the evening.

The following day, an old friend, the father of two small children, came to visit and we talked about the experience of becoming a parent. 'It changes your whole life,' he said, with a complacent smile. I disagreed fiercely with this banal observation. Changes, I took him to mean, one's central aim in life, so that in his case he no longer thought of himself as living for business success and personal pleasure, but for the happiness and future of his children. Understandable in a business man, I thought scornfully, but nothing fundamental had changed in my life; my conviction that I would one day achieve something worthwhile in the academic world was as strong as ever; children would never be the centre of my life.

A delusion! But however much I may have failed to fulfil my youthful aspirations, and although I never did return to academic life, I have never lost the conviction that 'a work of my own' is an absolute necessity. Except for the first three years of Sarah's life, I have always had such a work. But of course Sarah changed my whole life. She brought happiness, responsibility, sharing, a new order in daily life, new intimations of the strength of the human spirit (hers). She changed my life in small ways and profoundly. It was through her that I learned to love and to accept love, not in the excitement of falling in love, but soberly and enduringly. She had already changed me, but I did not know it.

During the early winter we had been preparing to move into a new flat on the ground floor of the Victorian house where we lived. It was twice the size of our basement flat, and its high-ceilinged rooms had large windows. Encouraged by my mother, we had taken it on a seven-year lease and set about modernising it. Erwin watched with a meticulous eye, pointing out to the builder floorboards not screwed down, and patches of old paint incompletely burned off, until relations became very tense. I shopped for kitchen equipment and furnishings, wanting everything to be well made, handsome, timeless and good value. Years later, returning to London after an absence in Australia that had been shadowed by many griefs, we looked at the white walls, the natural-coloured curtains, and the charcoal-grey carpets. 'It was all done with such optimism,' Erwin said. Yes, a blind optimism, not based on any clear idea of the life we might lead, with no apprehension of the possibility of tragedy, inspired simply by the conviction that we were blessed by fortune.

But as moving-day loomed, I became profoundly depressed over this creation of a permanent home, my first.

I brooded on the contrast between fragile human flesh and solid brick walls which would outlast us all, or which, alternatively, would be our tomb when the Bomb went off. I reflected that we were wilfully destroying a snug happy existence in the familiar small flat, that whether we moved or not, the birth of a child brought us closer to the front of the procession to the grave, that Erwin might die before me and leave me to carry the responsibility of parenthood alone. I have a record of these forebodings, because in the attempt to restore equanimity, I reverted to the habit of talking to myself on paper. One terror is absent from the closely-typed pages – that Sarah might die before me. But I asked, 'Does Sarah know about death?' and replied, 'Childhood is not the time for knowing about death.'

After the gloom of anticipation, our first months in the new flat stand out as particularly happy. Besides relishing the large sun-filled rooms, I was sharing with Sarah the exhilaration of a new stage in growth. Repeatedly during her infancy, there were days when she was discontented and fretful before a new leap forward, as if bored with practising her previous discovery; then, with the conquest of a new skill, would come a surge of joyful energy. I echoed her moods. The latest achievement was sitting up. I bought a high chair, which raised her to our level, and she became an equal member of the group gathered around the kitchen table.

Cecily and I were sitting there, talking about her and, of course, singing her praises while she watched from the high chair, smiling contentedly. Cecily commented, 'It's not food that is the primary need. It's admiration.' Putting her hands to her forehead, she bowed her head to the table three times in a mimic of hieratic reverence, chanting solemnly, 'We worship thee, O Goddess! Accept our homage, Beautiful One!' Sarah laughed with delight, keeping her eyes on Cecily so as to miss none of the adulation.

Cecily asked if I would like to join a discussion group for young mothers which met in Hampstead, under the patronage of an eminent psychoanalyst. At any other time I would have accepted at once, pleased and flattered. Instead I calculated the distance to Hampstead, glanced at Sarah's glowing face and declined. 'I don't have any problems,' I said apologetically.

We laughed with Sarah often; her gaiety was infectious. Yet I thought that sometimes our laughter made her uneasy. A bewildered shadow seemed to pass over her face, and her eyes looked questioningly into mine. 'I think being laughed at is one of the most terrifying experiences,' I said to Cecily on one of these occasions. 'Oh, but this is loving laughter,' she replied reassuringly. This time I was not reassured. Although our laughter always brimmed with love and admiration, it seemed to me that the line between laughing with and laughing at is a fine one, impossible not to cross unwittingly. Shared merriment can change into one-sided amusement at some saying or gesture which emphasises a child's smallness, or powerlessness, or ignorance. With overflowing tenderness, we watched her discover and interpret the world, but we watched from a vantage point different to hers, and what we saw could not always be shared.

I have forgotten the incidents in Sarah's life which prompted this reflection, but I did record one during the childhood of her brother Daniel. He was older, about three, and 'fishing' in the kitchen with a stick and a piece of string. 'I caught a flathead!' he shouted in triumph. The string was cast again. 'I caught a schnapper!' After another cast, 'I caught a barracouta!' And then, 'I caught a smoked eel!' Of course we laughed, but I felt on his behalf an incomprehensible and wounding ambiguity in our laughter.

Often, while I talked to Sarah, she would gaze intently at my face, and sometimes, as I in turn watched her, she seemed to be trying desperately to speak. With a look of yearning on her face, her body tense with effort, making little movements towards me, and fixing her great dark eyes on mine, she forced from her throat broken gurgling noises. I thought that although she couldn't yet master the shaping of sound, she understood what it was to reach out to another person through speech, and that, without perhaps wanting to say anything in particular, she was trying passionately to utter a sound that would be more than sound.

Sarah now had her own room near the kitchen. When I put her to bed in the evening, soon after six, she usually fell asleep almost at once, and slept soundly until eight next morning. She rarely cried in the night, then or later. On evenings when she didn't immediately fall asleep, I would sit with her, pushing the cradle to and fro while I improvised a meandering lullaby, then bringing it cautiously to a halt while I waited to see if she opened her eyes. If she were still wakeful after several repetitions of this cycle, I would often take her back to the kitchen, where I held her on my knee, playing with her and talking, until she became quiet and appeared ready to accept that the day had ended.

Dr Spock and some of our friends disapproved. 'You'll spoil her,' they said. 'She'll get into the habit and you'll never get her to bed,' implying that sleep is disagreeable, a burden or a punishment, which a child must be trained to accept. But sleep when tired is an ease and a blessing; we didn't expect her to rebel against it simply because sometimes it didn't come to her at a time convenient for us. In fact no habitual battle of wills developed over bedtimes. Often it was some extra social excitement that kept her awake. She was always lively and involved in the presence of other people, whether me or a larger group. She never fell asleep in company, as most children do, including her brother. As a baby, she never slept in my arms, except a few times in the car. Even at this early age, she seemed to need an interval of transition between sociability and withdrawal into sleep.

Occasionally the transition took a very long time. She had been put to bed and taken up again several times, staying in the kitchen until she looked exhausted and nothing pleased her any longer. I rocked the cot for what seemed an eternity, but each time I stopped she began to cry. On one of these evenings, as I sat in the near-dark pushing the cradle away from me and pulling it back again, I noticed that I was acquiring that essential maternal attribute, patience. You wait, often performing some repetitive act which neither absorbs nor satisfies, but which prevents you from doing anything else. You know that waiting will not be endless; eventually the child will sleep, or learn to open the door, or grow out of the passion for fishing. But it takes longer than you had imagined it could, far longer, so that you stop thinking about release and simply sit and push.

'Patience is a virtue,' we used to say when I was a child, mockingly, since it didn't look much like one; and I didn't claim virtue in this. Patience was taught by self-interest. If I didn't wait until she slept, she would cry herself into a rage, I would have to get her up yet again, it would take even longer, and perhaps leave scars of despair that would destroy our peace on other nights. The quickest way to regain my own freedom was to wait. So I was thinking of myself as I sat there, but not only of myself. I suffered with her fretfulness, longed for her sake that she should find the peace of sleep, and even while I chafed for release, felt grateful that simply by sitting there and pushing the cradle, I could do something for her.

Twice a year, before Sarah was born, I had gone to Paris to buy for the family firm. I see from a note written while I was pregnant that I had looked forward to continuing these visits. Now, as spring approached, I thought longingly of the beauty of Paris, of good meals and the pleasure of looking at chic new clothes, of freedom and challenge, and I knew that it was all beyond my reach. I could not leave Sarah. I was too aware of her dependence and trust; the image of her tear-stained face and frightened eyes when I didn't appear was too vivid. Such intimations, rather than any theoretical conviction about bonds of attachment, made me abandon the idea of travelling without her, and until she was four years old only childbirth and illness ever separated us for more than a few hours.

But the pleasures of being alone at home with her had begun to pall. I felt imprisoned and imposed-on. Resentment boiled up into a tirade against everyone and everything. I poured out on paper my rage against Erwin for retreating to his studio, against visiting relatives for regarding me simply as housewife and provider, against Sarah for keeping me from interesting work, blocking the trip to Paris, and making endless mess. 'I feel ill and tired, and it's all someone else's fault,' I wrote, although I knew that such outbursts help only by revealing their absurdity. But I resolved to get away, to get into the car and drive off. With Sarah of course; it did not occur to me for a moment to leave her behind. I would have liked to start that instant, but I could see that her needs demanded some preparation. By the next afternoon, I was ready to pack both of us into the car and set off, heading for a country hotel that someone had recommended.

An hour later, I sat in a teashop in Henley, already soothed by overhearing other tea-taking ladies admire Sarah's competence in drinking her glass of milk unaided, and by contemplating an ancient sunlit brick wall on the other side of the street. The hotel, though, was shabby and forlorn, in a kind of country I particularly dislike, cow-country, flat, treeless and damp; they gazed morosely at us across the river. Next day we moved on. I drove all morning, stopping only to buy food for lunch, and at midday sat in the car under leafless dripping trees, while I fed Sarah out of jars, and munched my dry sausage rolls, not knowing where we would be at nightfall. But I enjoy the traveller's illusion of homelessness, and she was an easy companion, sleeping in the cot while I drove, and, when I stopped, sitting beside me in the car-seat, alert and cheerful.

Late in the afternoon, after several fruitless enquiries, we came to a rambling, but this time welcoming, country-house hotel with a big garden, near Bath. We stayed there for several days. The sunny weather returned; it was even hot in the winding valleys. Each morning I tucked Sarah into her pushchair (I had chosen one which could be flattened to make a narrow bed), parked it in a sheltered corner of the garden, asked the barmaid to keep an eye on her, and with blithe confidence went off to walk in the country. All went well; I returned at her usual waking hour, and each day I got back just as she was beginning to stir.

I walked again in the evening. When I put her to bed in our bay-windowed room, unable to rock her to sleep because I had left the undercarriage of the bassinet at home, she cried, and I listened outside the door, in distress. But very soon there was silence, and in the last hour of sunlight I walked beside a derelict tree-lined canal, or climbed streets of stone houses with flowery gardens above the winding Avon.

The afternoons were more difficult. I drove to Longleat and she cried all the way, though I tried to reassure her with an improvised song, 'Cheer up snoo, we'll soon be there, we'll very soon be there!' But the sight of the great house in its bowl of park and woodland lifted my spirits. We had tea on the terrace in solitude, and she sat, delighted and unafraid, while a peacock strutted close to her. The next afternoon I pushed her chair along a tarred road to the village half a mile away, bought baby-food, inspected the church and gazed longingly at a meadow path too rough for us to negotiate, after which there was nothing to do but return the same way, recognising how much worse the tedium of home would have been without Theo to look after her, and without a car for the occasional escape.

For the last two days, Cecily joined us. We went to Longleat again, and this time Sarah slept in the car. As we drove along the road where I had sung to her in desperation, I turned my head to look at her. 'She's still there!' I said to Cecily. 'Of course she is,' Cecily replied, amused. 'Did you think she might have vanished?' It seemed too foolish to admit, but that is what I had briefly imagined. I did not yet understand how deeply her life was fused with mine; my acceptance of her was still mixed with astonishment. I half expected that a creature whose capacity for giving and receiving joy I had not anticipated might disappear as suddenly as she had come into being. I can't chart the fading of this sense of precariousness, but that was the last time I remember noticing it. Four years later, she had become so indissolubly part of my being that I did not conceive of living without her.

I returned home, restored by new sights and country peace, and it was a long time before the furies of resentment overtook me again. The summer was coming, visitors arrived, we planned a holiday abroad, and Sarah learned to speak a few words. My journal, kept up for a little longer, became more sober. I see that I embarked on some solid reading, attended two scholarly meetings, and thought about looking for a job. 'But not just yet! Perhaps by September.'

And why had it taken me so long to rebel against a home-bound, baby-centred existence? 'I had been wondering how long you could stand it,' Cecily said to me at Longleat. My revolt had nothing to do with any fluctuation in my love and concern for Sarah, which increased steadily throughout her lifetime. I thought at first that the answer was quantitative – I could stand so much monotony and no more. Now I see an obvious explanation. It was when I was pregnant or nursing that I changed into another self – passive, accepting, unreflecting. Sarah was ten months old when I stopped nursing her; revolt against the housebound life followed almost immediately. Other women have written about their resentment at this domination by biology. I resented it so little that I didn't even recognise it until I began to feel embarrassed at writing about this passive mother who was somehow myself. I still share her enthralment with Sarah, but her inert acceptance of a confined domestic existence now seems utterly alien.

The few days near Bath were my last opportunity for many years to enjoy country walks. Soon afterwards, Sarah's pattern of sleeping changed, and there were no more quiet mornings. Mrs Theobald would look after her for an hour or so, but I never dared ask for a whole afternoon so that I could drive into the country and walk. So I had to accept another consequence of motherhood, being hobbled to a child's pace and tethered by a rope no longer than her span of endurance.

I never talked to Sarah in conventional baby language, but there was a time towards the end of her first year, when I improvised my own. I used to run out of things to tell her, now that she was awake for so much longer, and instead I talked to her in strings of nonsense syllables: 'Chip chip chip chip my sweetheart; croom croom croom; choodle choodle choodle!' The habit added to our family vocabulary the word 'snoo', derived from a Goon Show refrain. 'Snoo: a species of vigorous independent small animal; a child with these characteristics.'

A tradition-hallowed moment came when we heard her speak her first word. Since then, I have reflected on the uncertainties which must cloud our identification of this first word, if it can be said to exist, and tried to imagine what sort of experience it could be for a child to utter it. I can see that the transition from babble to speech is more elusive and harder to understand than parents want to believe. But no contemplation of these mysteries has destroyed my wishful conviction that the first words we heard her speak were true words, which she understood and offered to us.

There were in fact two first words, one for me and one for Erwin. To me, while I was dressing her to go to the park and telling her what we would see on our walk, she repeated, with a dazzling smile of anticipation, 'Walk!' To Erwin, stretching out her hand towards a rose in a glass on the table, she said, 'Flower!' We were both charmed by the first words she gave us. Each seems particularly appropriate to the one who heard it, gifts which, if we had been granted the powers of the Good Fairy, we might have bestowed upon her. I, student and traveller, might have give her a longing to explore the vastness and variety of the world, and heard her echo in acceptance, 'Walk!' Erwin, artist, might have given her sensitivity to its visual beauty, and heard her exclaim in wonder and delight, 'Flower!'

Having invented this interpretation, I can no longer believe it was just by happy accident that we heard those particular words. But did we, influenced by our own desires, select, from her early experiments with sound, words that touched us deeply? Or did she, already recognising and responding to our particular individualities with that sensitivity to others which was characteristic of her, choose words which she knew would please us? It seems almost possible.

V

Summer in France

Before Sarah was born, I had feared that a child would put an end to the improvised wanderings in France and Spain and Italy which Erwin and I had loved. During our last holiday together, when I was already pregnant, I had savoured each resonant sight and smell as if I should never again experience the quiddity of some briefly encountered fragment of time and place. In fact we travelled with Sarah, and later with two children, almost as much, and almost in the same way, as before.

Memories of our travels have proved particularly enduring. Strangeness gives contours to events, making small happenings stand out, which at home would be swallowed up in the ordinariness of daily life. Perhaps also Sarah sometimes responded to the stimulus of new surroundings by flaunting new achievements, and occasionally, amidst so much excitement, by abandoning achievements already established. But often what I recall is not something she did or said, but just that she was there, in a fragment of the world transfigured by her presence. Vivid settings seen only once have preserved moments when I was sharply and thankfully aware of the miracle of her existence. I cherish every one of these memories, but ration my inclusion of them here, since their intensity is private and not shareable.

When she was fifteen months old, in the summer, we went to France by car. She still slept for a large part of the day. She had just learned to pull herself into a standing position, but hadn't yet stood alone and unsupported, and had scarcely attempted to crawl, much less walk. She spoke, but only a few words. So most of the time we simply carried her with us, adapting our habits so that her pattern of food and sleep could continue with as little disturbance as possible.

Travelling infants can use an astonishing amount of equipment, and for weeks before we left I was assembling it: new pushchair and car-seat, stronger and more compact than the first ones I had bought; bales of disposable nappies (at home she wore washable ones), involving visits to many branches of Boots to find enough of the brand that seemed best; new clothes for the beach; and, showing that we still retained expectations from the childless past, a large new tent to replace the primitive army tent in which Erwin and I used to sleep. Two nights in the new tent were enough to teach us that camping with a baby was an almost full-time occupation. We were not packed and ready to move on until past lunchtime. After that we stayed in hotels.

On our way south, to a rendezvous with Klaus and a stay by the sea, we stopped in Paris, and late on Sunday morning visited an exhibition of paintings by Poussin in the Louvre. Pushchairs were not allowed, so I carried her in, and since the gallery was almost empty, I put her down on the floor. Suddenly she became intoxicated by the vast expanse of smooth parquet receding all around her, and in that moment she achieved the conquest of space. Propelled by her hands and one leg, the other tucked beneath her, she scampered rapidly across the room, then turned and set off again, her face alight with pleasure and triumph. The handful of visitors seemed to share our exhilaration in watching her. Then I took her back to the hotel for lunch and sleep, while Erwin returned to Poussin.

As we drove on, we learned to divide the day into short segments: a spell in the car-seat between us in the early morning, a ride along some provincial pavement while we shopped for lunch, then an interval of sleep in her basket on the back seat, a long picnic lunch, and sleep again. We drove or stopped according to her needs, and so never visited the magnificent romanesque abbey for which we had made a detour, because just then she was tired; we drove on and have never returned.

In the late afternoon we stopped again to give her supper and make tea for ourselves. By experiment we found a hygienic basic diet for the holiday – bread, petit pois which she ate greedily, cold, from the tin, bananas, biscuits, and Evian water. Not an ideal diet, but a few weeks of it wouldn't do her much harm. One evening we stopped for this picnic in a little clearing away from the road. Sarah was sitting in her chair, already tucking into a tin of peas, and the kettle was on for our tea, when Erwin and I both chanced to go back to the car, out of sight, at the same time. Since she was a few weeks old, she had always accepted our temporary disappearances with equanimity, but now she began to cry, as if the absence of walls had aroused an archaic fear of being abandoned in the wilderness.

When we reached a hotel for the night, we put her straight to bed, and she fell asleep at once, so soundly that we went out for a peaceful dinner. We asked a maid or the porter to listen for her, but she never woke and cried out. In the morning though, she was awake much earlier than at home. I carried her over to the bed and we played with her there for an hour before we got up.

We had booked rooms in a small hotel where we had stayed before, on the coast near St Tropez, a square house backed by scrubby hillside. It faced a neglected garden and an avenue of palms lead down to the sea. Klaus joined us. It had not changed; even the resident families were the same, and they gave Sarah her first acquaintance with other children. Two small boys asked politely if they might give her a ride in the pushchair, and she laughed as they raced her down the path. They undertook to teach her to walk, and supported between them she took a few sagging steps, but whenever they let go she slumped to the ground. The elder boy came over to inform me solemnly, 'Elle ne marchera jamais!' A pretty girl of about four was less helpful. After watching Sarah's crabwise progress around the terrace, she went up to her and pushed her face firmly down onto the flagstones. The mother apologised. 'Elle ne comprend pas!' We thought she understood very well.

In the mornings I took Sarah down to the beach, often passing on the way a cheerful procession of children in red hats, who waved and called out to her. She didn't welcome the sea with the immediate enthusiasm that I, who had spent summers at the beach since babyhood and cannot remember learning to swim, had expected. She seemed afraid of the little waves which broke along the shore, and preferred playing in the dry sand. But when we visited two childless couples staying nearby, one of the men picked Sarah up and ran down to the sea; he bobbed her up and down in the water and brought her back smiling. Later in the day, while we were all sitting in a café, she started to grizzle and the other non-father entertained her by wheeling her vigorously round the streets.

An aura of privilege cast by her existence, mine to enjoy and to bestow, accompanied me much of the time. In the hotel, I washed her cotton rompers in the bathroom, under the notice forbidding guests to do laundry, and pegged them out behind the house, where the ground was stained with fallen figs. When I took them to the laundry in town to be ironed, I felt as if I were carrying a holy monstrance. 'C'est la dame de La Croix,' the girl at the counter called out when I went to collect them; so through her I had achieved a local identity.

I was scornful of anyone who did not appreciate her. One evening on the drive down, as our landlord was escorting us to our room in the hotel annexe, a dog ran past. 'Ya-ya!' Sarah called out. 'She calls dogs ya-ya,' I explained. 'That's what all children say,' he replied, bored. 'But she calls them ya-ya,' I repeated. Couldn't the stupid fellow understand that she didn't just say 'bow-wow', tediously, like all those other children, but had invented her own word?

Being with her, tending to her, were seldom less than

intense pleasures throughout the holiday. On later journeys, rage at unending chores and the lack of freedom occasionally engulfed me, but not then. When Erwin and Klaus tramped off together to paint, it seemed natural, and I felt only faintly miffed. They looked after her one afternoon while I drove into St Tropez. I set off jubilantly, but once arrived there was nothing I wanted to do. I looked through the racks of clothes in the shops but wasn't tempted to buy anything, and returned to the hotel before I was expected.

For her too the holiday passed serenely. There were a few small mishaps, an occasional rebuff, a couple of occasions when she couldn't fall asleep in the car, and we couldn't adapt our timetable, but had to drive on despite her howls. But for the most part she continued to live with lordly acceptance, eating when hungry, sleeping when tired, joyfully alert when neither. Nevertheless the accumulation of new impressions must have almost overwhelmed her. We noticed that her command of words gradually declined. By the end of the holiday, she was saying almost nothing but 'ya-ya', and whereas once this had meant precisely 'dog', she came to use it for anything that moved – cows, birds, bicycles, trains. Gazing through the window as the ferry left Boulogne, she stretched her arm towards the glassy, heaving waves, and called out, 'Ya-ya!'

VI

Almost Two

During her first winter, Sarah rarely left the shelter of house and garden. The bustle of the outside world had nothing to give her yet, and its noise and fumes could only do her harm, so I had never taken her out unless I had to. But during her second winter, I dressed her in a fluffy blue overcoat and brown corduroy leggings, and took her to Holland Park. I learned to race her pushchair across the main road, because the traffic lights barely allowed time, and no driver ever waited for us.

Surveying the world from her pushchair, she discovered that race of kindred beings, her age-mates. The children who had raced her down the path at La Croix were older, and she had accepted their attentions contentedly, as she did those of adults. Now, when she saw a child of her own age approaching in the street, her face lit up with recognition. As their pushchairs drew near, the two infants stretched out their arms in salute like emperors greeting each other from their palanquins, then turned their heads to keep each other in sight for as long as possible.

Through the wood I wheeled her, under the black trees that hid the surrounding city, picking a way between the roots; then down a narrow path, where once, in a parade of bravery I did not feel, I shooed away a gaggle of angry geese; across the lawn and through the flower garden, until we reached a previously unknown world, a terrace where mothers and grandmothers and nannies basked in the sun, babies slept in their prams, and a crowd of small children ran, climbed, tumbled and shouted. I sat and watched, and at first Sarah did too. There was a long interval between the discovery that she could stand alone and her first independent steps. At home she continued to propel herself around on her bottom, but not in the park. It was well into November, when she was eighteen months old, before she seemed about to abandon supporting arms and walk forward alone.

Time to get shoes for her, and we went one afternoon to buy them. The shop was crowded and we had to wait, standing in the aisle. Sarah, in her fluffy blue coat, stared at a small girl in a fluffy yellow coat who sat with short legs thrust out in front of her, surrounded by piled-up boxes and flanked by mother and shop-assistant in earnest consultation. Suddenly Sarah bent down and bit the white-clad toes which stuck up so invitingly. The other child howled, and we left the shop hastily, shoeless. That afternoon, Sarah walked for the first time alone, on bare feet red with cold, over the sharp gravel in Holland Park.

During the winter, Sarah learned to talk in complete sentences. Since then, I have pored over recent books about children's early speech, hoping to be reminded of how that astounding human ability revealed itself. Of course it is useless; it is not abstract theory or general description that I want, but to recapture step by step *her* growing mastery of language. The details have all vanished, leaving me with a sense of joyful awe at the plain fact of the achievement, by her and every child, but especially by those who, like her, become precocious talkers. Only two sentences from that winter have survived.

I had bought her a fleecy dark blue dressing-gown. She put it on, and studied herself in the bedroom mirror. 'It suits me, I think,' she said.

Erwin was laying vinyl floor-covering in her new bedroom. She walked across the sticky adhesive he had spread on the floor, and then across the hall carpet, leaving a trail of black footmarks. Erwin shouted at her crossly. She went quietly away, and returned carrying a spanner, which she placed in front of him, saying, 'Here you are, my Daddy.'

Of course she created her own versions of words: cuncacumber, lami, yerapples, tullis, cowool, cowool singer, lippish, carny, hopsly (cucumber, salami, vegetables, trousers, cotton-wool, cotton singlet, lipstick, cardigan, hospital). No doubt they were born of inaccurate hearing and immature pronunciation, but I also think that there was a time, before she divined the importance of rules, when she relished an exuberant creative freedom. We loved her inventions and adopted them ourselves, until about a year later, when she began to insist that we speak correctly. But I still say 'carny'.

I had bought a book for her already, for her first birthday, a children's encyclopaedia illustrated by colourful panoramas crammed with small objects. Peter and Iona Opie had pointed out that small children like small drawings, so I had avoided those first books with a few bold illustrations. *A First Encylopaedia* provided material for hours of pointing and naming things, and telling what they did, or said, or were used for. Now, as she learned to talk, we progressed to nursery rhymes. I didn't remember many from my own childhood, but I searched the books hopefully. Few appealed to me; they were too short, thematically irrelevant, too adult and knowing, lacking intensity, unmusical, a heap of left-over scraps. I didn't much enjoy reading them, nor she listening; she sat solemnly, with a dazed expression, and rarely demanded a repeat. Only one was a success:

> Sing, sing, what shall I sing?
> The cat's run away with the pudding string!
> Do, do, what shall I do?
> The cat has bitten it right in two!

I think she liked this because it amused Müttchen, Erwin's mother, who used to repeat it with a comic look of disbelief.

At the end of winter, we moved nearer to real stories, with the illustrated catalogue or litany: *Animal Babies, The Lion's Paw, The Animals of Farmer Jones*. Their literary merit was lower still, but they felt closer to the world she was living in. They appealed to the pedagogue in me. I remember reading and rereading them with pleasure.

When I went out without Sarah, I always left openly, saying goodbye and waving. Such frankness was not accepted by Mrs Theobald, and sometimes not by visiting friends either. They would distract her attention farcically, and wink and gesture to me to slip out unnoticed; or I would overhear them telling her that I had already gone. As if the pain of absence were concentrated in the moment of parting, and could be conjured out of existence by ignoring it; whereas to me, making a secret of departure would imply that it was ominous, and reinforce the terrors of absence. In her first years, Sarah always accepted my departure calmly, without crying, although I noticed, even before she could sit up, that if I were away longer than usual, she would be grizzly and petulant when I returned.

I still managed to have some time to myself, an hour or so in the morning, and again after lunch, while Sarah had a nap. I shut myself up in the big front room to read and make notes, reviving plans for research that I had sketched out before she was born. But there is a curious unreality about my view of the future. I believed that I would return eventually to sociology as a career, and imagined that I could re-establish myself through a brilliant piece of theoretical writing. But I made only the sketchiest attempts to discuss my ideas with anyone I hovered between two proposals, without plumping wholeheartedly for either, and I had no sense of urgency. The idea of looking for a job 'in September' had melted away; I now gave myself 'four or five years' for full-time motherhood. An eternity. I made no serious attempt to plan research that could be completed in that time, to help me re-enter the world of jobs and grants. In every vision of the future there is an element of fantasy, but mine was almost pure fantasy. But this was the expansive sixties. The prospects were not as bleak then as they would be now.

I have since come to believe that this illusion

contributed enormously to the continuous joy of Sarah's life. It masked the conflict between career and maternity. My terror of sinking permanently into domesticity faded, and I began to look on those four or five years as an interlude of legitimate irresponsibility, like a holiday. Instead of feeling anguish as time and opportunity slipped by, I continued to cherish an image of myself as a career intellectual, while devoting most of my time to her. Reading and making notes gave me mental stimulus without the strain of trying to manage parallel lives. But when, while writing this book, I began to perceive how much strength I had drawn from delusion, I was astonished, having hitherto accepted the dogma that only those whose lives are grounded in reality can act beneficently towards their children.

Although I shut my eyes to the future difficulties of returning to a career, I had come to know the bouts of exasperation and boredom familiar to housebound mothers. The sessions at my desk were short, and all too soon I would hear Sarah calling and knocking at the door. I had to let her in, and we would be alone together in the winter gloom, I shaken by the interruption and not immediately re-attuned to her pace. I envied Erwin the quiet of his studio, and sometimes rang and begged him to come home. But I never tried to reorganise our lives so that I would have more time for writing and study. When my brother-in-law André, a dedicated scientist, visited us in the summer, he was astonished that we looked after her entirely by ourselves. How could we spare so much time from our own work? Why didn't we get a nurse? I don't remember what reasons Erwin and I gave him. I only recall our certainty, mutually acknowledged then and confirmed between us since, that we couldn't deprive her or ourselves of the happiness that grew from being constantly with her. I feel it still. I admire today's career mothers, I didn't stay home so constantly with Daniel, or with Sarah when she was older, but whatever I regret in my own past, I have never regretted devoting those first two years so completely to her.

My token return to intellectual work soon petered out, because by the end of the year I was again pregnant, placid and contented. From the start I had hoped that Sarah would not be a solemn only child, and at first I thought of the new baby primarily as a companion for her. I didn't debate about when, ideally, this second child should appear. Dr Adler urged us to make it soon, and we were lucky not to wait long.

Since the baby was due in the summer, we decided to have an early holiday and go to France again at Easter. I imagined us settling in to a small hotel in Touraine, with delicious food and perhaps a garden where Sarah could play, and we left in cold mid-March to find this Eden. The afternoon ferry from Folkestone was almost empty; we had tea beside a window, watching the seagulls swoop over the grey water, with Sarah, very lively, sharing for the first time the excitement of departure.

We had bought yet another piece of equipment, a collapsible cot with silky net sides and a turquoise-coloured rim. Nowadays the shops are full of ingenious and attractive baby gear, but this had just arrived in Harrods from

America, and I felt as though it had been made especially for her. It had to be folded and strapped onto the roof of the car every morning, and at night unloaded and set up, usually in the bathroom, so that she could have a room to herself. Some of those country bathrooms were enormous. In retrospect it all seems very laborious, and I watch without envy as travelling parents manipulate equipment even more complex. For me, then, this small task, like countless others performed for her, was suffused with purpose and pleasure. Through the work of caring for Sarah, I came to know a relationship which has almost vanished from the western world, but which once suffused every level of society – that of serving with love. It has become not just rare, but despised, so that a friend who read this chapter urged me to cut out the word 'serving', as if it were obscene. But 'serving' is what I mean, and it is one of the gifts I received from her.

Before the holiday, Sarah had usually settled easily to sleep, and I had assumed that this would continue while we were away. On our first night away from home, in a small country inn where we were the only guests, I tucked her up in the cot, drowsy and contented, before we went down to dinner, but when I went up to check, she was crying. I put on her blue dressing-gown and brought her down to sit with us while we finished eating. The second evening followed a similar pattern. On the third, her protest began earlier, while I was unfolding her cot in a room with ferocious wallpaper and a narrow partitioned-off bathroom. She worked herself into a paroxysm of sobbing that took a long while to calm. After that, we took her to dinner every night in pyjamas and dressing-gown, and she shared our soup before I put her to bed. I think of that evening as a crisis of adaptation to change. From then on, for the rest of her life, she accepted every unfamiliar room and strange bed with the imperturbability of an experienced traveller.

The habit of reading a bedtime story started during this holiday. In a small bookshop in Tours, I bought for myself the latest volume of Simone de Beauvoir's autobiography, and for her a book of handsome animal pictures. I discovered that it could ease the transition from daytime sociability to the isolation of sleep. After tucking her into bed, I would lean awkwardly over the side of the cot, holding the book where she could see it, and describing the pictures to her. After a very few minutes, her eyes closed.

There was another change of habit. At lunchtime, instead of picnicking in the country, we looked for a town park, having learned that Sarah usually encountered playmates there. In Holland Park, other children kept to themselves, but in the parks of France they immediately drew Sarah into their games. In Loches, in a garden by the river, she disappeared with two little girls, and we heard their laughter from behind a bushy thicket; in Tours, on a sheltered terrace outside the art gallery, she played with a doll proffered by a small black girl; in Bourges, a circle of children beckoned her to join their singing game. These intervals of companionship were relaxing for us and must have given her relief from the weight of unremitting parental attention.

On our first trip to France, Sarah had lived essentially as she did at home. The second one was a voyage of discovery, and her guidebook was *The Animals of Farmer Jones*. She already knew the names of the farmyard animals, and what they 'said'. Now, one after another, she came upon their living presence. Rousseau, that intuitive poet of childhood whose empathy surprises me even more than my own (I at least lived with children), makes a rare mistake on this point. Emile was not to learn from books anything he had not first experienced in reality. But Cecily commented that this discovery of the correspondence between symbol and reality exhilarates, from whichever side it is made.

Already on the first morning, she woke up to see, from our bedroom window, a muddy farmyard populated by chickens, ducks and turkeys. Later, in Angers, in front of the Dames de France, she discovered a small donkey with an ungroomed coat, whose owner sold lavender. She stroked its shaggy side gently, touched it tentatively on the nose, and was so reluctant to leave that Erwin waited patiently beside her for almost half an hour, while the midday crowds pushed past, and she stood entranced.

After that we watched out for donkeys. We saw one looking over a gate, but when Sarah and Erwin went to offer it some bread, it retired to the back of the field, to her great disappointment. It was named the Shy Donkey, and she talked about it for years. A second donkey did consent to eat some bread and Sarah, somewhat fearful, asked to be lifted up to touch its nose. Demands to 'Touch donkey!' 'Touch cow!' 'Touch horse!' (reluctant to be touched, most of them), punctuated the succeeding days. Another refrain, which we found very moving was her farewell to these creatures: 'Bye-bye cow!' 'Bye-bye horse!' 'Bye-bye flowers!'

In the yard at the back of the hotel where we stayed longest, among the crates of bottles and the broken chairs, were rabbits in a wire-netted cage. She used to run downstairs in the morning to visit them and to converse somehow with the proprietress, who gave her lettuce leaves to feed them. The only creatures she didn't want to go near were some huge pigs, grunting and squealing in a muddy, stinking pen. And when we passed a lonely farm where geese waddled beside the road, she was asleep, and I have been left ever since holding a gift I could not deliver.

Her encounters with the animals of Farmer Jones reached a climax while we were picnicking at the edge of a field. At the far corner, coming towards us, appeared a tractor driven by a man in blue overalls. 'Farmer Jones! Farmer Jones!' Sarah called out excitedly. Our laughter was certainly loving, but once more I felt that it was unwittingly treacherous.

My dream of a smiling country inn proved illusory, and most hotels informed us that they had been booked out for Easter months before. We finally settled in Richelieu, a model town built by the great Cardinal for the workers on his estate, in the middle of a wind-swept, water-logged plain. The hotel was on a vast empty square; its public rooms were austere and the food plain, but we had a big room with a low-beamed ceiling and an antique high-chair, in which Sarah sat for breakfast. It felt homely.

Our friend Marie-Pierre joined us there, and each

morning we walked in the seigneurial park, where the elm avenue was just coming into leaf. We nodded at the large French family who were our fellow guests, and noted the contrast between Sarah's noisy exuberance and the sedate composure of the French children. In the park, she ran around and talked incessantly, while they walked decorously beside their parents. At night, Sarah's voice resounded through the dining-room, calling out finally as I carried her to bed, 'Goodnight Daddy! Goodnight Marie-Pierre!' and to the poster of a Gallic rooster by the door, 'Good-night cock!' We agreed that the subdued behaviour of the French children at dinner could well be preferred to Sarah's noisy pleasure, but not if it meant scoldings, punishments, and the disappearance of her visible joy in living. And indeed, sour admonishments echoed from the other table.

But on special occasions she could conduct herself with charm and dignity. On Easter Sunday, we indulged in a grand lunch at a restaurant high above the Loire. In the car, Sarah and Marie-Pierre sang nursery rhymes, Sarah chanting a version reduced to its essence: 'Baa-baa sheep! Wool! Yes!' Just before we arrived, she fell asleep, and remained sleeping in the car while we drank an aperitif in the sun and waited for a table; then, refreshed, she sat quietly beside us while we ate our way through six courses. I thought proudly that she understood the proper behaviour for the occasion.

And I felt indignantly protective when others did not credit her with such understanding. During a visit to Marie-Pierre on our way home, Pierre watched Sarah as she walked towards his handsome antique desk, and warned her sternly not to touch it. She burst into tears, and Pierre, bewildered, asked, 'What is the matter with her?' Sharing her sense of being misjudged, I replied, 'She is like everyone, she doesn't like being scolded.'

Sight-seeing during this Easter was for me even more restricted than on our first holiday. While Erwin visited cathedrals and galleries, I waited outside with her. I couldn't go for a walk after lunch, although Erwin would stay with her, because she refused to take her nap in the back of the car, and we had to drive off, soothing her to sleep through movement. But morning walks through ancient towns, and afternoons driving through the landscapes of early spring could not fail to bring moments of intense pleasure: a farmyard smelling of dung and rain-washed grass, where speckled guinea-fowl pecked by the roadside, and a pear-tree in full flower shone in the late afternoon sun. Being there with her.

VII

Waiting for Daniel

We decided to get an au pair girl to help after the second baby was born. She would have Sarah's room, the most private in the flat, and Sarah would move to the room opposite ours. Her new room didn't need much furniture. She had already graduated from the bassinet to a drop-sided cot, given to us via acquaintances, by an unknown family who no longer needed it. In the centre of the room we hung a Japanese lampshade, which she named 'moon', after she had seen, one night, the full moon lying low in the sky. 'Touch moon!' she commanded Erwin and he would lift her onto his shoulders so that she could reach the paper globe. The only other item I thought essential was a low chest on which to change and dress her, as Jennifer had taught me. We searched the second-hand shops, and Erwin found a handsome red mahogany one for £3.

'I don't think you should wait till the girl is here before moving her into the new room,' Cecily advised. 'Two important changes at the same time could muddle her idea of cause and effect.' So we started to use the room as soon as it was ready. Even so, Sarah became suddenly demanding and restless at bedtime, and we invented a first ritual. Each of us paid a formal goodnight visit, in which the same stories and gestures were repeated. Every night she asked me for a drink of water, which I didn't think she wanted, and I mimed turning on a tap, filling a glass, and carrying it carefully to her. Stories were not yet out of books but had to be improvised. I strained my exiguous gift for invention, but usually fell back on recounting the events of the day. In that hopeful summer it seemed natural to begin, 'We had a lovely day, didn't we?' A few years later she would climb on my knee to demand, 'Read we had a lovely day!'

I am sure I told Sarah quite early about the new baby, but I remember little of the telling. An image recurs, of her sitting on top of a small cupboard in the bathroom, while I stood in front of her doing up her cardigan, with the optimistic revelation hovering between us. Not much to be recovered from that! But I know I found this sharing of a secret, as no secret had ever been shared with me, a special pleasure for both us.

Dr Adler proposed enthusiastically that I have the second baby at home. We discussed it in the bedroom. 'The bed is too low,' I pointed out. 'We could raise up the legs on telephone books,' he suggested, lifting a corner of the divan to demonstrate. It would have needed ten telephone books per leg. I decided to go back to the Marylebone nursing home.

Meanwhile life with Sarah at its centre flowed on into summer. Before she was born, I had anticipated having to live in a child-scarred home like those evoked in modern novels, with scribbles on the walls, gobbets of food encrusting the furniture, and toys strewn over the floor. My sister Betty's house had never looked like that, but tidying, washing and organising filled her days to a degree I could not emulate. But Sarah never scribbled on walls or smeared food on furniture, and her few bouts of destructiveness were short-lived and specific. At one time she got a wild pleasure from pulling books out of the bookcases; at another from ripping up cigarettes. We countered by avoidance, leaving the lower shelves empty, putting cigarettes out of reach.

Her feats of memory surprised us. Standing in front of a bookcase full paperbacks, and putting her finger on the spine of *King Solomon's Ring*, in which, the year before, I had shown her its tiny drawings of dogs and birds, she said 'Ya ya book!' Seeing from the kitchen window a man walk up the path, she said 'That's Mr Preston,' naming the insurance agent who called on Mrs Theobald once a month. 'We're going to Daniel Neal's to get you some new shoes,' I told her. We had been there only once, six months earlier. 'Can I have a ride on the rocking horse?" she asked immediately.

She began to stay up a little longer when friends came to dinner. She always loved meeting people, and dinner guests broke the confining narrowness of family life. I could not feel that I was unwarrantably imposing her on them. If they didn't want to see my child, let them stay away! I wouldn't have inflicted on Sarah the rebuff of showing her she wasn't wanted.

New tenants moved into the studio at the bottom of the garden, a young couple with a big dog, a monkey and a five-year-old daughter, Arabella, who became Sarah's first friend. They played together in the garden and Sarah visited the studio constantly. She developed a huge admiration for Arabella, giggling at her jokes and watching her acts of defiance with open-mouthed wonder. Arabella's parents gave Sarah an outgrown rocking-horse, which she rode strenuously in the garden, making her hair bounce in rhythm.

I read her first real story, *The Tale of Jemima Puddle-Duck*, in an old copy which Theo gave me; I had never heard of Beatrix Potter. Sarah listened with flattering attention. I remember its small square pages, the delicate blues and greens, and the theme of disaster narrowly averted, but it was only when I re-read our disintegrating copy recently, that it seemed a curious book to offer a two-year-old, with its esoteric detail about a vanished rural society, its sexism, its coy hints of hidden menace. But she did draw from the story of Jemima a meaning which retained its power for her: the fox, reappearing in other stories, and soon joined by the wolf, was a creature both fascinating and threatening, metaphor for danger and death.

Now that she could follow a story, scanning the rack of Little Golden Books in Whiteley's became the chief pleasure of shopping. At first I used to elaborate the stories until they were three times their original length, both to savour my own virtuosity and also because I noticed that they were often too compressed for her to follow. Later, as her skill in listening increased and my zest for improvisation waned, I was more likely to abbreviate. She never, then or later, insisted that I stick rigidly to a text. And reading aloud was always a great pleasure for me; I was astonished when other parents complained that it was boring.

Occasionally I bought books that were too difficult for her, often out of impatient nostalgia for my own childhood. Belloc's *Cautionary Tales*, *The Magic Pudding*, and the *Nonsense Poems* of Edward Lear were all flops. I persevered longest with Lear, convinced that she must soon appreciate his lively rhythms and incantatory repetitions; but she listened passively to my spirited renderings, and I had to acknowledge failure. However she did like a little book of Lear alphabets, in which her favourite was:

E was an Eagle
Who sat on the rocks
And looked down on the fields
And the faraway flocks.

I had to read it over and over again, puzzled at her choice, until one day she repeated it after me, introducing a variation:

. . . looked down on the fields
And the faraway fox.

We knew nothing about how to find an au pair, and seized on the first opportunity we heard about by inviting Varenka from Zagreb, whose friend already worked for friends of ours. I went to Victoria one afternoon in July to meet her. Varenka arrived two hours late, clinging to the arm of a young man she had met in Calais, unapologetic and in tears. I swallowed my annoyance at the long wait and tried to comfort her, took her home, showed her the room which I had made attractive with new curtains and cushions, and accepted, touched, her gifts of salami and slivovitz. But the feeling of suppressed mutual grievance with which we began pervades the memory of her entire stay.

The au pair system flourished (and for all I know still does), because it half served the needs of both mothers and girls, but I never knew anyone who did not feel intense relief when the last au pair departed. Their innocence of household skills, the time spent in teaching them, or the guilt of giving them only the simplest and most tedious of jobs (ironing was almost the only useful thing that Varenka ever did), on one side; homesickness, the uncertainties of a strange country, and (at least in her case) lack of interest in other people's children on the other, made it an unsatisfactory relationship. Because there were no clearly-established conventions about how much work should be done, both sides felt exploited. Even worse were the obligations implied by the phrase 'au pair', as if a young niece had come to stay and share the pleasures and duties of family life. Nowadays we don't even ask our young nieces to stay for longer than a day or two, but under a pretence of equality we tried to live in close intimacy with a stranger separated by age, language and custom.

Varenka was a sombre, pasty-faced girl who tripped around on high heels and complained endlessly about conditions in her homeland. She never uttered a word of thanks or showed a sign of pleasure in anything I did for her, determined, she told Erwin before she left, not to catch the ridiculous English habit of perpetually saying, 'Thank you.' Her stay with us was short, ending with a row with Erwin while I was in hospital. Of course, she had been unhappy too. 'The whole time I was with you, I felt I was in prison,' she told Erwin. We might have learned to do better, but we didn't try again. Meanwhile she lived with us and did the ironing, and a bit of baby-sitting.

Again I waited without impatience for the end of pregnancy, my somnolence lightened this time by Sarah's gaiety. On summer afternoons we sat by the open French windows and I sewed, or read to her. The favourite story that summer was about Smokey the Bear's search for a lost fawn. I elaborated on Smokey's climb up the mountain to question Snarler the Mountain Lion, who merely growled, and said, 'Go away!'. One day I asked Sarah what Snarler had said. 'Have a peanut!' was her version. Cecily made a comment that had not occurred to me: 'Clearly going away is a tender subject.'

Klaus came to tea one afternoon and took photographs: of Sarah standing in the doorway with an expression of open-mouthed wonder; laughing as she forced the rocking-horse to a wilder gallop; caressing her cheek with my fur hat; of Mrs Theobald bending solicitously over her; and of Arabella running naked across the lawn. And my favourite photograph of Sarah and me together, sitting on the balcony under the sticky branches of the lime tree that overhangs from the next garden. She hides the vast curve of my belly and my face radiates happiness. The photograph has taken to itself a title from an old ballad and a poem by Auden, 'Underneath the Leaves of Life.'

The new baby was in no hurry to appear. Twice I packed books and baby-clothes, told Sarah I was going to the hospital for the baby to be born, and disappeared. Twice the attempted induction failed, and I came home next morning, cumbersome as ever, clutching the flowers that Erwin had bought in anticipation, without a baby.

They were the first nights I had spent away from Sarah, and although I worried about her, I relished the escape from responsibility. On the second occasion, after dinner, there being no sign of the baby's imminent arrival, I asked if I could go out for a walk. 'Good idea!' Dr Adler said. 'It might bring on labour.' That was no part of my motive; I simply wanted to make the most of my independence. I walked through the empty West End streets, elated by solitude and by the deep sapphire of the darkening sky, feeling an intense awareness of my individual existence, and an optimistic openness of expectation like that of arriving alone in an unfamiliar city.

After the second attempt to induce labour failed, I said firmly that I would now wait until the baby demonstrated its own willingness to appear. Two more weeks went by before I was awakened one morning by the traditional pains. Daniel was born at nine that night, again without instruments or drugs, and in time for Dr Adler to catch the second half of his concert. The day this time felt almost ordinary. 'You seem very competent,' the nurse said, as I lay on my side pushing the pain away with long slow exhalations. She told me next day that she had never seen a natural birth before, and I felt a certain triumph at being able, at the age of forty-one, to give a professional nurse this experience. Had she said 'competent', or was it 'confident'? I felt both. At the end I was aware of a reminiscent fear that my body might be torn or cut, and of holding back a fraction of strength, but again the moment of birth was sudden and brief. 'It's a boy!' I heard a nurse call out. 'Are you sure?' I asked. 'Quite sure. He's got a little tassel.' Lying in bed next morning, I felt sufficiently pleased with myself and the world to think that perhaps we should have a third baby.

I had told Sarah that I was going away for the baby to be born. Each time. Though what I said on returning home with empty arms I don't recall. I had also told Theo that Sarah knew the reason for my absence. Despite this, Erwin overheard her telling Sarah, 'Mummy's gone shopping.' ' The false beginnings, postponements and lies (for Sarah of course knew that I hadn't simply gone shopping) must have been bewildering for her,' I wrote much later. No doubt. But after trying to imagine how she might have experienced those weeks before Daniel's birth, I see that even without those false starts, she would not have had much idea of what was going on. At other times, I believe that I often heard and replied to her unspoken fears and questions, but for the big events in my own life, Daniel's birth, and, later, my mother's death, there were silences which I was too preoccupied to notice.

Familiar with theories about sibling rivalry, I had been afraid that she would be jealous of the baby. Cecily recommended a device thought up by a friend of hers, that of presenting her small daughter with a doll and a doll's pram, so that mother and daughter could look after their babies together, and the child forget jealousy in pride at her own motherhood. I resolved to follow this example. Perhaps, though, I never really trusted it, because I didn't make careful preparations, but bought, at the last moment, an ugly doll with an over-sized head, whose wardrobe consisted of a skimpy nightshirt furtively run up on the machine. I hid the doll in my suitcase, together with a collection of small toys, which I planned to give Sarah each day when she visited me in hospital.

She came with Erwin the next afternoon. I heard her footsteps in the corridor, and her clear voice calling out, 'I want the baby!' When the nurse brought her tiny brother, she became the first member of the family to hold him in her arms. She sat gazing down at him with a expression of love and tenderness. The doll and the collection of bribes remained in the suitcase.

Erwin stayed with Sarah as much as he could while I was in hospital, knowing that he, more than anyone, could reassure her. He brought her to visit me every afternoon. She greeted me perfunctorily, scarcely looking at me, not wanting to be cuddled or to talk. She climbed experimentally onto the bed and then ran off to explore the corridors, returning with a rose given her by another patient. The visit was usually interrupted by a session of temperature-taking, the baby's feed, and the doctor's call. Sarah and Erwin were dismissed from the room, and went off to do shopping, or to walk round the neighbouring streets, returning to relate what they had seen. I hoped they would not get back while I was breast-feeding Daniel, as I thought Sarah might resent it; but one afternoon she came bouncing into the room before I could ask them to wait. She showed no obvious concern, or even interest, beyond asking what I was doing. From then she seemed to take my nursing of Daniel cheerfully for granted. Once, back at home, she asked if she could have a suck. I said that the milk was for the baby and that she too had been given it when she was tiny. When Daniel was put on the bottle, she wanted to try, and I gave her one, but she soon handed it back.

One afternoon, on their way home, Erwin and Sarah stopped to feed the swans in Regent's Park, and one of the birds, snapping at the bread Sarah held out, bit her finger so that it bled. She was very frightened and cried loudly. Erwin explained that the swan had not meant to bite her, but couldn't take the bread because she held it with her fingers instead of on her outstretched palm. He always had patience and understanding in soothing the children after a disaster, and in finding an explanation which would turn it into an everyday misfortune. By the time they visited me next day, Sarah had mastered the story of the swan, and told me about it excitedly. A little later I chanced to borrow from the library a book about a small boy who was bitten by a donkey when he offered it sugar. Sarah asked to hear it again and again, laughing each time at the boy's cries of pain and outrage, and at the blood on his hand. The story of the swan, often retold, remained part of her personal epic. More than three years later, Daniel would occasionally announce solemnly, 'The swan bit Sarah!'

The homecoming with Daniel felt very different from

that with Sarah. Then we had returned to the temporary shelter of a furnished flat, in a mood of pure celebration, scarcely knowing what it was we were celebrating, pleased with ourselves and infatuated with the baby, but still wearing the identities of our irresponsible past, and oddly incurious about our future with her. Now we came back to a home of our own which we had worked to create, with a high chair in the kitchen, baby food in the cupboard, nappies hanging to dry in the laundry, and newly-established habits, which had continued while I was away. I carried Daniel in, and put him down on the bed, knowing where I was.

VIII

Illness

A few weeks later, on a glowing autumn morning, I dressed in town clothes to visit Dr Adler for a post-natal check-up. Standing before the mirror, I thought that I looked surprisingly young and radiant. When I told Sarah where I was going, she said, 'I don't want you to go to the doctor, he'll make you sick.' From the height of my conscious good fortune I replied, 'Doctors don't make you sick, darling. They make you better. But I'm not sick. I'm going so that Dr Adler can see how well I am.'

But while the doctor was prodding my stomach, I felt an odd slithery sensation, as if something had broken through a constraining barrier. On the way home, I was assaulted by pains so severe that I could barely manage to drive, and once there I went straight to bed. The pains became sharper and more preoccupying as the day went on. Not steadily though; I remember getting up and making myself a thick ham sandwich. It is a banal fact about this other life, that a mother is lucky if there is someone to look after her children when she is ill; only in an acute crisis can she expect to be looked after herself. Theo and Varenka saw to the children, and Sarah stayed away from me, as she always would when I was ill.

When Erwin came home, he immediately rang the doctor. The evening brought other unusual events, and this time no-one attempted to explain them to her. First Dr Adler and then an unknown man disappeared into my room and shut the door. They emerged looking solemn, conferred in low voices, and made telephone calls. Theo put Sarah to bed, and when she awoke next morning, my own bed was empty.

Dr Adler and the surgeon he consulted had diagnosed a burst ovarian cyst, necessitating an urgent operation. They found a room for me in the nearby clinic of Saint Vincent de Paul, and I was taken there that night, unable to walk, and carried vertiginously down the front steps in a garden chair. Dr Adler discussed with the Sisters how I could continue to nurse Daniel, and optimistically proposed that Erwin should bring him to me each time a feed was due. But it was soon apparent that this would take up Erwin's entire day, and instead, Daniel was installed in an empty room next to mine. The Sisters obviously enjoyed looking after him, and, I suspect, deliberately kept his room vacant. 'His analyst won't know what to make of that,' Cecily commented, looking at the starched white coif soaring over Daniel's head.

After the operation the two doctors urged me to agree to a course of radiotherapy, which would destroy any remaining malignant cells, but also the possibility of having more children. Still floating in the beatitude of new motherhood, I was astonished by their grim faces; it would not have occurred to me to reject their advice. I have since understood that they did not rate my chance of survival highly, although no-one said so then, and I felt no pang of fear, even when Dr Adler commented 'They've learned an immense amount in the last few years. These new treatments have a success rate of thirty per cent.' I didn't apply this figure to my own fate, but considered it with detachment, like a statistic in a research report, before replying, 'I don't call that particularly good!'

Erwin brought Sarah to visit every day. Once, meeting Dr Adler, Sarah tugged at his trouser-leg, demanding, 'Give me a kiss!' He looked surprised, hesitated, and then bent down and kissed her. The Sisters regaled her with biscuits and took her off to see the fishpond in the garden. When she left, I waved goodbye from the window, trying to make everything seem normal and acceptable, no cause for alarm. Outwardly she remained her ebullient self, but one afternoon she ran off to visit another patient and returned to announce in a strained voice that there was a weasel in her room. 'No, darling,' we assured her, 'there couldn't possibly be.' But she insisted that she had seen it, and when someone went with her to investigate, she pointed to a furry shape under the bed, a slipper. At the time I saw this merely as evidence of her truthfulness. If she said there was a weasel, then there was – something, anyway. Now I recognise the weasel as brother to the wolf and the fox.

This illness was probably the most traumatic event of Sarah's life. She demanded to hear about it over and over again. 'Read you went to hopsley,' she asked, even several years later. There were two stories about hospital. 'Do you want I went to hopsley to have Daniel, or I went to hopsley to have an operation?' Nearly always it was the latter, and she listened intently while I repeated every detail I could remember and thought politic to tell her. I usually lost interest in a repeated story long before she did, but this one, because I was aware of her deep involvement, kept its vibrancy for me too.

When the pathologist's report was received, I was told to stop breast-feeding Daniel immediately, and this sudden weaning showed me how directly the processes of reproduction inhibit intellectual liveliness. Three days earlier, when my consent to radiological treatment had been sought, I had not asked a single question. Now, out of hospital, I searched the Public Library for books on radiotherapy, and acquired a knowledge of the half-lives of various substances. I was to be given an injection of radioactive gold, which has a short half-life and becomes harmless when its curative work is done. A photograph of a small figure lying under the outstretched arm of a faceless metal monster was my preparation for the follow-up cobalt therapy. It was more informative than anything the doctors told me, and so rather reassuring.

Before I was due at the Royal Marsden for the gold injection, I had two weeks at home. Klaus again took photographs, this time of Sarah with Daniel. She leans solicitously over his cot. 'Don't cry, baby! I'm here,' I heard her say, as I left the room to prepare his bottle. When I returned, she tested the temperature by shaking a few drops onto her wrist, as she had seen me do, displaying that sense of maternal responsibility that the trick with the doll had been intended to encourage, but now it sprang from human reality. It was the beginning of a love for him, in which her sense of superiority as the elder gradually fused with awareness of their common citizenship in the child-world. Already in the nursing-home she had called him 'my little brother', with pride tempered by condescension. No doubt there was hostility too, but it did not take the form of violence or dangerous threats. 'I'm going to smack baby,' she would say, but it was mock-serious, and I don't think she ever did.

I asked Klaus to take a family group that I could send to my mother. In order to include us all it had to be deliberately posed, not Klaus's style, but he agreed to try. The result is not noticeably formal. Sarah threw herself boisterously around in Erwin's arms, and sucked her thumb. Daniel, unlike Sarah in photographs at that age, is not smiling, but stares solemnly at the camera, as if the preceding weeks had taught him already that life presents disasters which must be faced stoically.

Because I would be a radiation hazard, Sarah was not allowed to visit me in the Royal Marsden, but I arranged for her to accompany me when I entered the hospital, and to see my room, thinking this would help her to believe in my continuing existence. I talked to her on the telephone every day too, but her voice sounded strangely thin and reedy, and she said little.

Varenka left while I was in hospital, and we had no more live-in help, although Theo continued to lend a hand, and a daily help came two mornings a week. Even with this assistance, looking after two children seemed to consume more than twice as much energy as looking after one. I also had to attend the Royal Marsden five days a week for radiotherapy (efficiently organised, but the journey took time), and once a week for the Consultant's clinic, (unpredictable, and usually I had to wait for several hours). So no time for any gesture towards sociological study, and I felt no compulsion to try to make time. But I continued to believe that I would return to academic life – at some vague future date.

The hospital gave me tablets for the nausea caused by radiotherapy. I kept them in a drawer, where I also hid the red-and-yellow lollipops we sometimes bought her at Sainsbury's, and the tiny silver cachous faintly flavoured with peppermint that Cecily used to bring her. Climbing on a chair to get these, Sarah found the anti-nausea tablets and helped herself. I found her staggering around, flushed and giggly. She told me immediately what she had eaten; only one, she said, and because I knew that she could see from my expression that I was seriously concerned, I believed her. One wouldn't do much harm, the hospital thought, only make her drowsy; no need to worry, unless we couldn't wake her. For twenty-four hours she alternated between sleepiness and drunken hilarity.

Perhaps my faith in her truthfulness will seem rash. The gravity of the situation might alternatively have elicited guilt and denial. Certainly in my own childhood, as far back as I can remember, I would have lied if caught like that. But Sarah had never seen Erwin or me suddenly transformed by anger or rejection. She had no fear of us and so no compulsion to lie. I believe still that I could trust her absolutely.

We read a large number of stories that autumn, many borrowed from the Public Library, where I had taken out tickets in her name. Sarah listened to them all, but few became even temporary favourites. Not those charming tales full of knowing jokes, written with an eye on the adult reader. Not even Babar. The stories that made her laugh were simpler, such as that of *Harry the Dirty Dog*, who played in the mud and refused to take a bath. I think now that there were too many stories and too much mediocrity. Perhaps I am nostalgic for my own childhood, when no-one read aloud to me and I was given few books, but read those few over and over again, especially *A Child's Garden of Verse*, and a small anthology of stories from Grimm and Anderson. Some of those I read to Sarah did come to have a strong resonance (at least for me), my favourite being *The Little One*, a fable by Dare Wright about solitude, doubt and family happiness, illustrated by lyrical photographs of its doll heroine and her living playmates, turtle, butterfly and crow.

In November, Arabella and her parents left the studio in the garden. It was not the first disappearance in Sarah's life, but the first of someone she had loved. Wanting to allay the bewilderment and desolation I thought she must feel, and to preserve her confidence in the stability of the world, I set out with Sarah to take Arabella a Christmas present, a copy of *The Little One*. At the address Theo had been given, a tall Victorian house in Kensington, the woman who opened the door did not know the name – perhaps at the top flat! We climbed the shabby stairs, but no-one answered the bell at the top flat, and I felt that I had unwittingly confirmed the mystery of Arabella's disappearance.

Erwin's sister Ruth stayed with us for several weeks at Christmas. She held Daniel's clinging monkey-body close to her own, when he woke up and we brought him into the kitchen. 'Il est charmant, le petit neveu,' she told her husband, André, on the telephone. 'Nephew' surprised me. I had not thought of Daniel as a nephew and this unsentimental word was transformed into a term of endearment by her voice. As 'brother' had already been by Sarah's use of it.

One wintry afternoon we went with Ruth to feed the geese at Kew, as we had often done on summer evenings before Daniel was born. That day, the park was deserted, a freezing wind blew from the river, and the sky was a sullen yellow. The geese hissed and ran towards us with outstretched necks, seizing the bread, and pulling at the pockets of my coat. I hastily threw them the remaining bread, hoping they would have the sense to know there was no more, while Ruth retreated with Sarah. We walked quickly back along the towpath, and drove home with heightened pleasure at being together.

It snowed at Christmas and again in January. We awoke to find street and garden blanketed in flawless white. Snow in the city has never lost its enchantment for me, who never saw snow in my own childhood. I dressed Sarah and took her down to the garden, expecting that she would be captivated by the transfigured world and its possibilities for play. But she scarcely looked at the snow and listened absently to my exclamations.

For some time we had planned to visit Australia in the New Year, to present the children to my family. And there had come to be another reason. My sister Betty had written to say that our mother's cancer had recurred, and that there was now no possibility of cure. So when I booked a flight for us at the end of January, I did not book a return. I thought we might be away for as long as six months, but it was five years before we returned to London, and Sarah lived half her life in the country where I had grown up, a country of the New World and its vast open spaces.

IX

Going Home

Every year during my childhood, at the end of January, my mother, or one of her sisters, or two of the three of them, left Australia for London and Paris on a buying trip. They always talked of 'going home', although they rarely saw any of their English relatives. We, their children, were still at Portsea, the seaside resort at the bottom of Port Phillip Bay where we spent the summer holidays. So we did not go to Port Melbourne to see them off, but instead waved goodbye with bed-sheets and towels, from the end of Portsea pier, as their ship, Orient Line white-and-yellow or P&O black-and-ochre, steamed past, on a sea already darkened to sombre indigo.

On their return in August, mid-winter in Australia, they used to leave the ship at Adelaide, and take the overnight train which got into Melbourne on Sunday morning, leaving the wardrobe trunks and deckchairs to follow, but bringing their most prestigious purchases with them. An extended family was waiting in the misty cold as the train drew into Spencer Street Station, and then everyone drove home to our place. Over tea and hot-buttered toast (a mid-morning treat sufficient in itself to mark the occasion as special), the suitcases were opened, and new garments displayed, tried on, admired, analysed with professional acumen, and heaped opulently on the floor, together with silk scarves, and new-smelling handbags, and heavy glass necklaces, and gold-thread pullovers. There were presents for us children of course. At first toys from Paris – once a mechanical bird in a cage which chirruped and flapped its feathered wings – and later, clothes for us too, unlike any worn by our schoolmates: the first beach pyjamas, and the next year, when everyone was wearing beach pyjamas, the first grey flannel slacks and blue blazers with brass buttons. The careless extravagance of those homecoming mornings gave the travellers an aura of magic.

At moments during our own journey to Australia I had the illusion of re-enacting such a homecoming. We travelled in quite another style to our usual one, with a limousine to take us through the wet dark London streets to the airport, and first-class air-tickets, provided by the family. No wardrobe trunks, but fourteen pieces of luggage, including the bassinet with its undercarriage roped inside. I wore a new coat and a frivolous pink-and-white Paris hat presented to me by a wholesaler. We were taking presents too, gifts for the family – and the two children.

The long flight, which usually reduces one to stuporous exhaustion, slipped by agreeably. First-class space and service helped, as did the six stops (nowadays reduced to one) which allowed us to breath fresh air and move our stiffening limbs. But chiefly it was because I was always occupied, talking to Sarah, reading to her, helping her to find something she would eat from the succession of meal trays, which I had described to her as a treat in store, but which, to my disappointment, she eyed very languidly. And preparing Daniel's bottles, feeding and changing him, sorting out clothes for the varying climates, packing and repacking our cabin bags.

Daniel, in a cot slung on the bulkhead in front of us, lived an almost normal existence. He cried at the change of pressure at take-off, but otherwise fed and slept, and gazed amiably about as I carried him on and off the plane. Sarah didn't sleep during the entire journey. After Singapore we were give a spare seat so that she could lie down at full length, and she might have slept then, had I not give her a sedative, which I had asked the doctor to give me 'just in case'. Instead of making her drowsy, it stimulated and irritated her; she threshed about and arched her body like a fish in a net, while I wiped her damp forehead and cursed my lapse of trust in her ability to sleep when tired.

After two nights and a day we arrived in Darwin, and then continued on to Sydney, where we transferred from International Arrivals to Domestic Departures, and hung around for several more hours because the Melbourne plane was delayed. The children endured it all cheerfully. We finally landed in Melbourne, thirty-six hours after leaving London, at four in the afternoon, the hottest hour of a blazing summer day.

Because of our late arrival, only my sister Betty was waiting for us. Suddenly I felt very tired, from the journey and the blazing sun, which beat down from an incandescent sky onto bleached summer paddocks. I sank onto a chair, clutching Daniel, while Erwin reclaimed our luggage. Betty bent down and spoke to Sarah with an easy complicity which won her instant confidence, and they walked off hand in hand. I rested in blank passivity, already enjoying that bounty of home, unstinted help given without asking.

The journey was not quite over. We drove to my brother Bruce's house, to shower and change before another drive, 60 miles, and the final fatigue-blurred arrival at Portsea, where my parents waited.

The family reunion remained low-key because we all came down with flu. Betty sent for Dr Edwards from Sorrento, whom we were to get to know well. Sarah had a high temperature and diarrhoea, and although both subsided quickly, they left her physically weak. A few days later I watched her try out her current gesture of high spirits, a kangaroo hop, and manage to lift herself only a pathetic inch or two from the floor.

Summers at Portsea had been the happiest times of my own childhood. Every year, for the eight weeks of the summer holidays, we had moved to The Grange, a gabled and bow-windowed limestone residence from the 1890s, which gazed out to sea through a gap in the row of pines at the bottom of the garden. It had a brick-paved courtyard with a well in the centre, from which water was drawn by a squeaky iron pump; cooking was done on a wood-burning range even when the temperature was in the nineties; the dining-room sideboard held glasses etched with Greek-key borders, shiny green plates embossed with vine leaves, and a heavy ceramic cake dish which housed the slowly eroding cliff of dark Christmas cake. On cool afternoons, when we came home from the beach, we were each given a piece for tea.

We children, three, and sometimes four or five of us, shared a bedroom and a bed under the central gable. We hung our bathers to dry on the balcony, and when they fell onto the corrugated iron roof beneath, risked getting stung by bees, which lived under the balcony floor. In the large neglected garden, formal paths outlined with white stones were overgrown with bunny-grass. A great flowering gum tree sheltered the carpeted tent in which Aunt Nell slept, away from the noise of the house. At the end of the holidays, after the tent had been taken down, when the summer residents had gone home and the beach was deserted, it came into flower. Usually we saw only the first clusters of buds lifting their lids to show the tightly packed stamens, but once or twice we carried home a vision of the tree flaming in vermilion splendour, solitary and immense under the hot sun, haloed by bees.

After my cousins left school, the summers in The Grange came to an end. A little later, my mother bought a place of our own at Portsea, not another picturesque dilapidated limestone mansion, as I had coveted, but a newly-built weatherboard house with a modern kitchen and a reliable hot-water system. It had great beauty too, not in the house but in its setting. The land at the edge of the cliff was just wide enough for a narrow terrace with a white fence like a ship's rail, beyond which was the sea, in whose presence we lived. Through plate-glass windows, it dominated the living room; my mother could look down from her bed through twisted ti-tree branches into its green shallows; ships went past on their way up the bay; the dark line of the Queenscliff coast opposite broke into fragments with the changes of light; sometimes a faint glow in the night sky revealed the city at the head of the bay, and on a very clear day, its towers floated like a mirage above the horizon. During the year we were to live there with the children, each time I returned from the city and opened the gate, I felt a shock of exhilaration at rediscovering, beyond the white railing, the sea's shining presence.

This was the house to which we now returned. It had been extended by wooden outbuildings added wherever there was space, and after our arrival accommodated fifteen people. Someone gave up a bedroom to Erwin and me, Daniel slept in the bassinet, which could be put anywhere, and Sarah was allotted the front porch, closed-in by a canvas blind. It didn't seem to frighten her that she slept outside the house, separated from us by the front door.

My mother was already diminished by illness. She got up a every day, but she was stick-thin under her loose dress, and nearly always tired. Her expression was gentle and remote. I was glad she had come to England when Sarah was born, for she seemed to have receded almost beyond reach, so that the sight of her newest grandchild did not greatly move her; she smiled and tried to talk to the children, but as if it was a duty. She both knew and denied that she was dying, competently explaining aspects of her will, but also talking about what she would do when she recovered. More than once she said to me, 'I think I'm very lucky. I have six grandchildren, and they're all healthy wonderful children. Not many women can say that.' The modesty of this summing-up of a lifetime touched and appalled me.

My father immediately took to Daniel. He came to love Sarah also, but it was Daniel who at once conquered his heart, and at first he used to watch Sarah closely for signs of hostility towards her brother. He often took charge of Daniel in the afternoon, when my mother was resting and everyone else had gone to the beach. He pushed the bassinet tirelessly to and fro with his big hands, and sang the songs we had heard as children: 'O hush thee, my baby, Thy sire was a knight, Thy mother a lady, Both gentle and bright,' and 'Row the boat, row the boat, Gently down the stream. Merrily merrily merrily merrily, Life is but a dream!'

'There have been three baby boys in my life,' he told me. 'Ivor, Bruce, and now Daniel.' (Ivor was his nephew, who had lived with my parents when they were first married, Bruce was his son, and Daniel was the youngest of his four grandsons.)

The last time I had been at Portsea, seven years earlier, my sister Betty had been fully occupied in looking after her own children. Now she had become the unquestioned head and benevolent priestess of the household, doing most of the cleaning, shopping and ordering of meals with unostentatious efficiency and regard for everyone's tastes. On the cook's day off, she prepared an enormous casserole and left it ready to be put in the oven, before going down to the beach with a crisp shirt over her bikini and a matching bandanna round her hat, often taking Sarah with her. She nursed my mother and still found time to help me with Sarah and Daniel. She invited Sarah's companionship in all her activities, rocked Daniel in her arms when he was fretful, fed and changed him, washed enormous loads in the clanking and certainly not fully automatic washing machine, and took me shopping in Sorrento, telling me which brand of milk to buy for Daniel, where to find plastic sandals for Sarah, and lending me her wicker shopping baskets. When she thought Erwin and I needed respite from family, she gave directions for finding hidden ocean beaches, and lent her immaculate car. It was the only time anyone ever shared the work of looking after children in that generous and unassuming way which fosters no anxious burden of obligation, and which is rarely possible except within the family. It renewed our closeness as sisters, which had become attenuated when our lives diverged, she choosing nursing and then early marriage, I study, teaching, and exile.

There were four other children at Portsea (Sarah's cousins, aged between ten and fourteen), my sister-in-law Joan, and at weekends the two Bruces, my brother and brother-in-law. The final member of the household was Mrs Ramplin, the English cook, who had come to Australia to visit her daughter and stayed on, unhappily, constantly grumbling. She was untidy and slovenly, and not much of a cook either, but she and Sarah got on. 'Come here and I'll give you a cuddle,' she used to say to Sarah, who adopted the word. 'I want a cuddle and a kiss,' she would demand, with a sideways glance at me, having noticed that I didn't approve of Mrs Ramplin's talk. Sarah learned another phrase from her too, declaiming one very hot day as she struggled to strip off her t-shirt: 'I'm hot as a boiled egg!'

I have sometimes wondered how the drastic transformation of her world affected Sarah's trust and understanding of the world. Did it seem more incomprehensible than it did to us, since she possessed no explanatory scheme of time and space? Or did it matter less, since her own meaningful world, parents and brother, toys, books and clothes, moved with her. Confusing surely, yet I don't remember signs of disorientation. The new life was full of immediate interest, and in that densely populated household there was always someone to pay attention to her.

She seldom spoke about London, but remembered two beings clearly: Mrs Theobald, and Mrs Theobald's cat. When we left for the airport, she carried a little basket which Theo had given her; later she took it to school, always recalling that it was from Theo. But it was the cat she remembered most vividly. Two years later, I heard her confide to a group at her nursery school, 'I've got a cat in London. His name's Sooty.'

By the time we had recovered from flu, our presence was as much taken for granted as if we had been there for years. It was rather deflating, but the moment for ceremonies had passed, and it was only through these, vestigial as they were, that the family could affirm its bonds. There was seldom a straightforward expression of affection, or even interest. Indeed not much talk of any kind. In the daytime everyone scattered to the beach, before and after meals they sat with their heads in the newspapers, and at mealtimes dishing-out and clearing away went on non-stop. No-one said they were glad we had come, or asked about our life in London, my illness, or our future plans. Nor did they question Erwin about his life, family or work, but simply accepted him without curiosity. 'I suppose Erwin is Lutheran, being German,' my father once said – a statement, not a question. I didn't reply, and told Erwin only much later. He didn't accuse my father of smug self-deception, as he might have done had it been anyone else; by then he had come to appreciate my father's unworldly simplicity.

And why didn't I tell my father about Erwin's escape from persecution in Nazi Germany, or his arrival in Australia as an enemy internee, his work as a graphic artist, or his scattered family? Because I belong to that Australian family, and share its taciturnity even while I criticise it. And I don't regret my failure to reveal more of myself, or ourselves. It made for a dull but comfortable atmosphere. Occasional overtures to my mother in the past had left me in no doubt about the wide differences in values between our generations, differences which could be ignored if not spoken of, but which had stung my mother into fear, anger and hostility, on the few occasions when I had attempted to confide in her.

I do regret that I never questioned my parents about their own lives and families, to add to the meagre facts I had picked up when I was younger. For they never talked about their own past either. Perhaps it is an Australian characteristic. The historian Kathleen Fitzpatrick comments somewhere that those who migrated to Australia in search of a better life had little reason to recall what they had left behind.

We settled into the routines of an extended-family holiday. This time, Sarah took at once to the pleasures of sea and sand. I bought her a shimmering pale blue air-ring, and late in the morning we went to the beach by Portsea pier, where the water was deep and clear, and where I had learned to swim almost before I could walk. Supported by the ring, she floated in front of me, above the dancing reflections of sunlight on the sandy bottom. Then I dressed her in dry clothes before going back for a proper swim. Surveying the sparsely populated beach, she would announce, 'I'm going to talk to some people,' and set off confidently towards her chosen group. When I emerged again from the sea, I would hear laughter and lively chatter; calls of 'Goodbye Sarah' followed us as we trudged off over the sand.

On other days, she played at the water's edge, while I watched her from a few feet away. Often the sea was almost motionless, but one choppy day a wave knocked her over. I leaped up immediately, but when I reached her, she was lying on her back with an expression of mild surprise while waves washed over her face; she made no effort to sit up; she might have drowned without a struggle.

I was bathing Daniel in the laundry, a bare wooden cube flooded with morning sunshine and the song of wattle-birds from the surrounding scrub. Sarah watched, as she had done many times before. Suddenly she pointed. 'What's that?' 'That's his penis.' 'And what's that?' 'His balls.' She waited while I dressed him, and then ran ahead of us to the sitting-room. 'Daniel's got a penis and a ball!' she announced, excited and pleased, the bearer of important news. Unfathomable mystery, the repeated discovery in childhood of the same facts. Not only had she known Daniel's body from the start, but earlier, I remember her watching Erwin in the shower and riveting her gaze unmovingly on his genitals. This time, certainly, the rediscovery was fused with her accelerating conquest of language; observation gains stability when it can be put into words. But her triumphant announcement to the rest of the family seemed to be of facts, not words.

Erwin, Sarah and I set out for a picnic at the back beach, leaving Daniel with the family. We drove along a sandy track through the ti-tree scrub, and left the car just below the crest of the last dune. While we were looking for the path down to the beach, Erwin carrying Sarah on his shoulder and I following with the picnic basket, a black snake slithered out of the bushes and crossed the hot sand in front of Erwin's feet. We both started to run, spilling the contents of the picnic basket. By then of course the snake had disappeared. I doubt if Sarah even saw it, but it became an often-repeated story, of which she and Erwin were the heroes. Nearly two years later, Erwin painted a wall-panel for her, with characters from the stories he invented; she demanded that he also include the encounter with the snake.

I read out to Erwin a newspaper story about two brothers on a Gippsland farm, who had been running across a paddock when a snake appeared in their path. The elder leaped over it, but the young boy landed short and

was fatally bitten. I hadn't noticed Sarah's presence, but she overheard me, and for weeks continued to demand, 'Read about the snake and the two little boys!' I did as she asked, always following with another snake-bite story from the papers, in which the child victim was rushed to hospital, given anti-venin serum, and recovered rapidly.

Did it seem that we were in a country where death was an ever-present threat: death from drowning, from snakebite, from the bushfires whose acrid smell reached us across the water? I see it that way often now – a country, a time, a world, an existence. But then I felt no conscious terror. Children drowned certainly, but not if one were properly alert. I planned what to do if fire threatened the scrub near the house, but as an obvious precaution, not with any presentiment of tragedy. And if I kept my voice level when recounting the snake stories, and balanced tragedy with happy ending, it was to assuage her fears; I recognised none of my own.

A few weeks after our arrival at Portsea, the rest of the family suddenly packed up and went home to Melbourne, leaving us like jetsam on a deserted beach, unable either to return to London while my mother was perhaps only weeks from death, or to acknowledge that we were waiting for her to die. Still there seemed no reason why we shouldn't enjoy an interval of ease after childbearing, illness and travel. The sun was hot and the terrace overlooking the sea even more idyllic now that we had it to ourselves. Erwin set up a studio in the loft over the garage. I was content with the presence of the children, the routine of looking after them, and the nostalgic calm of a place scarcely changed since my childhood. I took Erwin and the children to see The Grange, deserted in the sunshine after another generation of children had gone back to school, and to Sorrento back beach, where the uninhabited coastline, blurred with spray, stretched as far as Cape Schanck, scene of long-ago picnics.

This peaceful existence was interrupted by a telephone call from Betty to say that my brother Bruce had suffered a cerebral haemorrhage and was critically ill. He died that same night. The pathos of my brother's early death is not part of Sarah's story but it had consequences which are. It changed the balance of forces within the family business, and plunged me into a fight over its control and survival. The enchanted isolation of our own small family ended.

X

Family Business

The family business was called Cann's, after my maternal grandmother, who had emigrated to Australia from her native Yorkshire with four young children in the early 1890s. Life in the first years was no easier there than it had been in England, and money was tight. Then, in about 1910, her three daughters (Aunt Mary, my mother, and Aunt Nell) started a modest dressmaking establishment. It had grown steadily and, after the end of the First World War, had blossomed with the new demand for fashionable ready-to-wear clothes. There were annual buying trips to London and Paris, and later to New York. Customers almost came to blows over copies of the Chanel models they brought back from Paris, Aunt Nell told me. Through hard work, brash self-confidence, and a flair for line and colour, the sisters expanded the business until they owned a department store in the centre of Melbourne, and a factory for 350 employees. Cann's became, at least in the eyes of the family, the leading, indeed the only fashion authority in Melbourne.

By the early sixties, though, things looked different. The rag trade changed radically after the end of the Second World War. Lively small new firms appeared, better able to keep up with rapidly changing fashions. The sisters were getting old and their tastes becoming ossified, but they insisted on sticking to the strategies and procedures which had succeeded in the past, often down to the most minute detail. They still ran the firm autocratically. Formal ownership of the assets had been handed over to the children of my generation to save death duties, but the sisters had agreed that as long as one of them remained alive, she would have absolute control. To the end of their lives, they kept supreme confidence in their own judgment and distrusted that of almost everyone else, especially of their children and their children's spouses.

By the time of our visit to Australia, the business was operating at a small but increasing loss, the shop looked dowdy, and the factory ran at a third of capacity. Mary (she didn't like being called 'Aunt') had died, and illness forced my mother to remain at home. Aunt Nell, the youngest, held dictatorial power, which she exercised with passionate involvement in details but indecisiveness over large issues, and without, so we of the next generation agreed, her old flair and sureness of judgment.

There were five of us in the younger generation: two Tronsons, Peter and Peg, who were Aunt Nell's children, and three Grays, myself, Betty and Bruce; Mary had been childless. All three sisters were affectionate and generous towards us, (I sometimes reflect that I was brought up by a triple mother) but they didn't credit any of us with capability or common sense. The two who worked full-time in the business, Peter and Bruce, were liable to have their smallest decisions peremptorily overturned – as, I might add, was everyone else employed by the Firm.

For years, we children had conspired and muttered together impotently, convinced that the business could not be saved unless Aunt Nell retired, but unable to confront her. Submissiveness was deeply ingrained in us. We had no great faith in each other, no natural leader, and no idea what we would do if we were suddenly to achieve power. We were split into two family groups, a division emphasised by Aunt Nell's accession to sole charge (she was wary of the consequences of there being three of us Grays against her two), and by the sisters' provision that power would eventually be divided evenly between the two families. In discussions, the Tronsons were represented by my cousin Peter since his sister Peg lived in another state and did not take an active interest. On the Gray side, my sister Betty also did not want an active role, and Bruce and I neutralised each other by being covert rivals with different qualifications. I was the senior but he was more familiar with the business. When Bruce died suddenly, I became the unchallenged representative of the Gray family interest.

That alone would have changed nothing. Although I had hoped that while I was in Australia we would be able to 'do something about the business', I had no tactical plans, and was half convinced that Aunt Nell had a right to destroy what she had helped to create. But chance twice came to my aid. I happened to be present when my cousin Peter presented himself publicly, unasked, as the future head of Cann's. I had no high opinion of Peter's talents, and his assumption of the right to represent my side of the family filled me suddenly with fierce and self-righteous combativeness. From then on, confrontation with Aunt

Nell was overlaid by a confrontation with Peter, which was not weakened by any taint of impiety, and sustained by pride and self-respect.

A second chance meeting was with a benevolent outsider, my cousin Ivor, that nephew of my father's who had touched his heart as a baby, and who now owned a flourishing textile firm in Brisbane. He had flown down to attend Bruce's funeral, and afterwards talked to me about the crisis in Cann's, urging me to intervene, and encouraging me to believe I could do so successfully. And he made a decisive first move. He suggested we drive to Portsea to visit Aunt Nell, who was still on holiday. We called on Peter, inviting him to accompany us, but he refused, fearing a row. Aunt Nell regarded Ivor with the respect she felt for all successful businessmen, and he succeeded in obtaining her consent to two unheard of moves – calling in a firm of management consultants, and inviting an eminent company lawyer, Oswald Burt, to be Chairman of our Board of Directors – an institution which had not previously existed. Ivor issued invitations to both of these before Aunt Nell could change her mind.

The consultants and the new Chairman were powerful allies in the cause of reform. Henceforward Aunt Nell's exercise of power would be exposed to public scrutiny, and restrained by a whole code of conventions – for example, that a decision formally approved by the Board could only be countermanded by the Board. The Chairman was there to see fair play.

I became a director of the Firm at the same salary as Peter. Aunt Nell recognised the justice of the appointment, but I had to fight for the salary, withstanding furious tirades in which she reviewed my qualifications with contempt, and ridiculed my presumption in equating myself with Peter, who had worked in the factory for twenty-five years. Her anger was formidable; it was one of her greatest assets; but I was sustained by the conviction that putting myself on a level with Peter was a conciliatory gesture. Finally the Chairman, of whom she was somewhat in awe, said, in his benevolent elder-statesman's manner, 'Of course they should be paid the same.' It wasn't an enormous sum; Peter and Bruce had complained of the family's stinginess for years; but it enabled Erwin and me to pay our living expenses while in Australia, including someone to look after the children while I was at work.

I sat in my mother's office and did whatever tasks came my way. As a member of the family, my right to be there was accepted by all the staff. My duties were not defined, but it was obvious that I must stay around and keep my eyes open, learn as much as I could, make up my mind on the proposals put forward by the consultants, carry out the tasks they assigned to me, and show enough intelligence and strength of will to make their cooperation seem worthwhile. The relationship with Aunt Nell continued to be crucial. Everyone was aware that she had the power to dismiss the lot of us. Some of the changes that came to seem imperative ran counter to her entire experience and temperament. Yet she also wanted the business to have a secure future. So there was often genuine and affectionate cooperation between us, as well as continuing hostility.

It is certainly no accident that I succeeded in

challenging the older generation of the family only when I had a family of my own. I remember talking to the head of the consultancy firm after he had discovered how unpredictable Aunt Nell could be, and begun to suspect that for once he might not succeed in his crusade against the irrationality of the family business. 'Supposing you fail?' he asked me. 'How could I fail against an isolated old woman when I'm thirty years younger and have two marvellous children?' I replied. The children gave me a confidence that, earlier, I had never known within the family, and seldom outside it.

So before the pleasures of domesticity began to pall for the second time, I found myself in the ideal job for the early years of motherhood – one that was challenging, new to me, passionately involving, and vital for our finances, but not morally oppressive (I had always rather despised business), and fitting for this interval of retirement from the pursuit of academic ambitions. And since the job was a family one, deriving from relationships that are indissoluble and, in our case, indulgent, I was relatively free to be with the children when I needed to be.

During the preliminary manoeuvres, we had continued to live at Portsea, but if I were to go daily to work, other arrangements would have to be made. Betty suggested that I and the children live with her during the week, in the back half of the rambling house in Power Street, Hawthorn in which we had grown up, and which had been divided into two self-contained flats after I left home. Betty and Bruce had postponed building a house on an attractive near-by plot of land overlooking the river, so that Betty could look after my parents, who lived in the front of the house. Erwin would stay at Portsea where, I thought, he would be able to do his own work as a painter, and I would join him with the children at weekends. It seemed an equitable arrangement. I would defend Betty's interests in Cann's and she would contribute by housing and cooking for us. I would get a nurse to look after the children during the day, but would have the reassurance of knowing that my loving and competent sister was there also.

I settled the remaining problems with uncharacteristic promptness. I visited several nursery schools recommended by Betty, and was offered a place for Sarah in the one I thought much the best, the Robert Cochrane Free Kindergarten. I added two months to her age so that I could say she was already three, a deception I am ashamed of when I think of the unbureaucratic kindness I was to receive from the teachers. And the first employment agency I telephoned sent me cheerful red-haired Janny, Dutch migrant and trained nurse, who was expecting her first baby and wanted a job less strenuous than hospital work.

On my first morning with Cann's, I left the children without a pang and got a lift with my brother-in-law at half-past eight in the morning. The routine of going regularly to town began with some crisis I have forgotten. Once an organisational problem is resolved, all those preceding schemes and arguments and conspiracies lose their air of importance. Much of the work I did then, if I remember it at all, now seems absurd.

XI

Weekends

That winter, our family life regained its intensity during the weekends at Portsea. On Friday afternoons I left the shop after lunch, laden with parcels, and farewelled by the staff on the ground floor. Aware of impersonating my bountiful mother of thirty years before, I walked up Bourke Street to collect the car from an expensive indoor car park. We had been lent my mother's last car, a powerful Daimler. At Power Street, Janny had the children ready and their clothes packed. With Daniel in his basket on the back floor, where for the first few months he slept soundly all the way, and Sarah in a car seat beside me, farewelled a second time by Betty, Janny and Grandpa, we set off.

Sometimes we stopped at a suburban shopping centre, where I left Daniel at our branch shop while I bought t-shirts and pyjamas for the children. Once I lost Sarah in the Mall, and was about to put an announcement over the public address system, when I found her again, in tears. 'Lost in the supermarket', I read recently, is one of the terrors of today's childhood. I bought shrubs in shiny tins, Special Offer Three for a Pound, and Daniel lay half-concealed under a quivering leafage of wattle, callistemon, oleander and broom. Or we stopped at a Government nursery for native plants, where

Sarah ran barefoot between the beds, and I asked advice about what would survive on the cliff-face, and bought seedlings wrapped in cylinders of bark.

For most of the way it was still possible to drive on empty back roads, past old-fashioned farms and stretches of bush. Once we stopped to buy apples from a cool-store and Sarah stroked the neck of a cow in the paddock alongside. Months later, passing the same place, she remarked, 'That's where the cow was!' and Erwin and I preened ourselves on another feat of memory.

I drove fast, trying to beat the standard time of an hour and a half, working off the frustrations of the week. When we emerged from the bush and rejoined the main highway, we could see the outline of the Bay curving towards our destination, and Sarah asked me to recite the names of the little seaside townships we would pass: Dromana, Rosebud, Rye, Blairgowrie, Sorrento. After she had been going to nursery school for a while, she would announce, 'I'm going to sing,' and chant, heavily and tunelessly, 'Hi-dee, hi-dee-ho, The great big elephant is so slow,' or, with prompting from me, 'The animals went in two by two!' We drove past Sorrento's narrow sandy beach and wooden bathing enclosure, unchanged since my childhood, and up the hill, skirting the park where the Butchers, Bakers and Candlestick Makers had held their annual picnics. A mile or so further on, I swung onto a sandy track, and stopped outside the paling fence which hid the sea. Almost at once Erwin appeared.

The house was being painted, and often there were several station-wagons outside. Sarah knew the names of the men, Mr Coker, Bill and Jack, and after she had hugged and kissed her father, she ran off to greet them. 'Coker', she called the Boss the first time, but Erwin told her she should say 'Mr Coker', and thereafter, solemnly, she did.

On Saturday morning we went shopping in Sorrento. We parked in the main street, outside Stringer's Stores, which had grown from the old-fashioned country store I remembered, into a modern supermarket. Sarah hopped out of the car and ran ahead of us to talk to Carol the cashier. She liked to choose tins of baby-food and packets of biscuits to put in the trolley, but she was circumspectly moderate and I didn't need to make many covert returns. Next we walked down the street to the greengrocer's. Once, she chanted a rhyme from an alphabet book I had borrowed from the Kensington Library:

T is for Tub.
In a Tub, one fine day,
A pig and a parrot went paddling away!
They steered with a clothes-peg,
And sang 'Oink! Olé!'

'Olé! . . . Allah!' The ancient cry of acceptance and praise echoes still for me from the winter-empty main street of Sorrento, Victoria.

At the greengrocer's, I first heard an exchange that was to be repeated often. 'What's you name, dear?' asked a lady in a baggy tweed skirt. Sarah told her, and asked in return, 'What's your name?' Tweed-skirt looked taken aback, and did not reply directly. Very few people did. They made coyly evasive comments; only rarely did anyone tell her name, or her age with Sarah's assumption of equality.

The shopping expedition often ended with a visit to the tip, a smelly smouldering plateau of anonymous rubbish beyond the last houses, separated from the ocean by scrub-covered sand dunes. If no-one else was there, a cloud of gulls arose squawking as we turned through the gate, but often a station-wagon would be backed up to the edge, unloading its brimming cartons. The better items – an old ice-box, an armchair with exposed springs, a child's potty, sheets of galvanised iron, old doors – were helpfully left at one side, away from the fire. When we were clearing the house before putting it up for sale, we discarded an immense rickety sofa, and were pleased to see next day that it had gone.

We drove back to the house, unloaded the shopping, and ate a quickly prepared lunch. 'La', Sarah called it, a meal at which Daniel sometimes ate 'yerraples' from a Heinz tin. These were the last of her words, which we also used until she abandoned them and insisted that we do too.

After lunch there was an interval of quiet. The children slept, Erwin returned to the studio, I pulled a chair close to the window so that I could look out on the shining sea, and settled down with a book. I left the lunch dishes on the table so as not to cut into the time I had for myself. The memory of how jealously I hoarded it is a convincing reminder of how little I had then – only this space after lunch and another after they were in bed at night, but I was too tired for much by then. At no other time of my life have I read so little. I didn't even belong to a library, but picked over the meagre assortment of books in the house, left behind by the previous owner, or given at Christmas and not thought worth taking home. Occasionally I bought a paperback from the Sorrento newsagent.

Often I had less than half an hour before one of the children woke up. Activities for the rest of the afternoon had to allow for giving them a fair bit of attention. Daniel was still too vulnerable and easily tired for drives or the beach. I tried going off with Sarah, leaving him asleep in Erwin's care, but invariably he woke and howled, and Erwin could only comfort him by rocking the bassinet ceaselessly, without Grandpa's patience, feeling victimised. We found a solution in gardening on the cliff, with Daniel looking on from the playpen, and Sarah keeping up a running commentary.

'The beauty of this place is it has no garden,' various members of the family had said. Certainly it didn't have much, only the cliff-face of sand and crumbling rock, held by a few clumps of ti-tree and strewn with rubbish that had been tossed over the fence. I collected bucketfuls of cigarette packets, sweet papers, broken toys and old torch batteries. The sparse natural vegetation was being choked out by a stringy pea bush with puce flowers and bilious yellow leaves, which I hated. We burned mountains of it in the sitting-room fireplace, where it flamed and crackled and spat, showering the carpet with sparks. Erwin and I invented a method of terracing the bare falls of sand with lobed ti-tree logs, and spent hours pegging them into place. I planted my seedlings, including, in memory of The Grange, half a dozen sturdy little flowering gums. They would need careful nursing, which they were unlikely to get, but the last time I saw the place, two of them were still alive.

We justified this work as preparation for selling the house. 'It's absolutely pointless,' my brother-in-law said. 'The people who buy it won't even bother to walk down the ramp.' We didn't believe him, though in fact they didn't. But it was only an excuse; in reality we felt a surge of uncalculating love for that scrap of earth, the first for which either of us had been responsible.

In the late afternoon, when the cliff was in shadow, we lit the fire and made tea, and I read to Sarah. I had brought some of her books from England, and in Sorrento I found more Little Golden Books. But what I read most often that winter was an anthology of poetry for children which I found there, among the postcards and holiday paperbacks. Gradually I identified from its three hundred pages, a dozen poems which she liked to hear repeated. Flipping through the pages, I rejected many poems as too long, or too abstract, or too alien to her experience. The rest I judged by her reactions. She listened to everything, and never said, 'I don't like that'. But when something particularly appealed, her expression became more intent and alive. She liked poems that were vivid, concentrated and dramatic; nature lyrics and poems of mood and contemplation did not attract her.

The greatest favourite, which I particularly enjoyed

reading to her, was a ballad by the nineteenth-century American poet Bayard Taylor. 'Read the wolf!' she would command, and I would read:

High up on the lonely mountains,
Where the wild men watched and waited;
Wolves in the forest, and bears in the bush.
 And I on my path belated.

The rain and the night together
Came down, and the wind came after,
Bending the props of the pine-tree roof,
And snapping many a rafter.

I crept along in the darkness,
Stunned and bruised and blinded;
Crept to a fire with thick-set boughs
And a sheltering rock behind it.

There, from the blowing and raining,
Crouching I sought to hide me.
Something rustled; two green eyes shone;
And a wolf lay down beside me!

His wet fur pressed against me;
Each of us warmed the other;
Each of us felt, in the stormy dark,
That beast and man were brother.

And when the falling forest
No longer crashed in warning,
 Each of us went from our hiding place
Forth in the wild, wet morning.

Sharing this poem with Sarah remained a particularly poignant memory, and for a long time I cherished the belief that she understood all its celebrations: of the untamed new-world wilderness, of solitary courage and the will to survive, and of the kinship of all living creatures. I was slow to perceive a simpler fascination, the appearance once more of the voracious threatening wolf.

At bedtime, after her shower and before putting on her pyjamas, or after, since she was always happy to strip them off again, Sarah would announce, 'I'm going to play Ladies!' This was a private piece of show-off, never performed if strangers were present. Naked except for a plastic shower-cap pulled down over her forehead, she pranced, leaped and twirled, in absorbed mimicry, perhaps, of a ballet dancer seen on Grandpa's television, before an audience of two entranced by her beauty.

We usually stayed at Portsea until Monday morning, when I left after breakfast. I dropped Sarah at the nursery school, where she would be picked up by Grandpa at lunchtime, before setting off for the shop by tram, feeling cheerful and equable. Once, when we were later than usual in getting away, Erwin accompanied us to Sorrento to do some shopping. It was a clear mild winter day, and suddenly it seemed ridiculous to rush back to town. With agreeable feeling of playing truant, we bought a picnic lunch, and drove to a part of the ocean beach where the dunes sloped down towards the sea, in a long fall of coarse sand smoothed by the wind. We sat close together in the sun, eating our lunch and watching the rolling lines of surf. The air blew clean from the ocean and there was no sign that any other person had ever been there. We were fifty miles from a city of two million people, but we seemed to be outside measured time and mapped space.

XII

A Death

Mama's strength was ebbing and her involvement with the world becoming more tenuous. On the day of Bruce's funeral, she had said to me, 'I can't believe it!' It is what everyone feels after a sudden close death, but I don't think she ever did believe it deeply and strickenly, perhaps because she knew that she didn't face years of being forced to believe.

On that day she had been dressed and sitting in the dining-room, but soon afterwards she kept to her bed. From then on, she had day and night nurses to look after her. When Daniel, who was never such a good sleeper as Sarah, woke up full of energy at two in the morning, I took him down through the dark cold house and left him with the night nurse, for the entertainment, I hoped, of both.

Mama was never left to endure extreme pain, and she slept most of the time, but when she was awake she was languidly sociable. And, as she had been all her life, excessively undemanding. She accepted Betty's nursing ministrations, but when one afternoon, no-one else being about, I helped her get out of bed to use the chamber-pot, she was distressed and repeated several times, 'You shouldn't have to do this.'

One evening I came home to find that she had reached another stage in the descent towards death. She was barely conscious and very weak, and seemed again diminished, as if the last vestige of personality had been obliterated. I asked Erwin to come up from Portsea and next morning rang the shop to say I wouldn't be coming in. But when I returned to her room, where she lay against the pillows, looking tired and frail, she smiled and spoke to me. I asked her if she would like to see the children, since they were what I had of greatest value to give her. 'Just for a little while,' she said cautiously.

I brought them to her bedside, and she stretched out her hand gave each of them a modest matriarchal blessing. Did she say, 'Be good, Sarah . . . Daniel!'? Or was it 'Be happy. . . ?'

She died in the evening, four days after her farewell to the children, while we were all gathered for the weekly dinner which the two households shared in the big front dining-room. The nurses summoned Betty and me from the table. Mama lay on her side looking very small, her mouth open and a bony hand stretched out in front of her, like a starved bird fallen exhausted from the sky. The two nurses laid out her body, obliterating the look of life frozen in mid-breath, and turning her into a respectable corpse.

In the morning, Betty and I performed our last practical service for her, removing the clutter of medicine bottles, basins and towels, and cleaning and tidying her room. We put roses from the garden on the dressing-table and then, looking together at her body, covered only by a sheet on this cold winter morning, we took a fleecy blanket from the wardrobe and put it over her. 'She hated being cold,' Betty said, with an apologetic smile.

Sarah was not drawn into any of this. Janny came every day as usual, and the children's life went on at the back of the house. I did not tell her about Mama's death or funeral, and was not even aware of the omission until years later. Yet the week of the death was full of unusual happenings for her. On the day Mama's body was to be taken away, not knowing what else to do, Erwin and I went to the nursery school and stayed for the afternoon, sitting on the steps in the winter light, and watching the children play. Then, before the funeral, Sarah and Janny watched while Betty and I tried on an assortment of hats sent out from the shop, giggling and making disparaging comments. Suitably hatted, we disappeared for an hour, returning accompanied by a crowd of female cousins and elderly family friends, to drink tea in the dining-room where, because of my mother's illness, there had seldom been visitors. Later we were joined by the men in dark suits and black ties. Clearly something out of the ordinary was going on, but if she was puzzled, I did not notice.

We drove back to Portsea the same night, the four of us enclosed in winter darkness, glad to be alone again in the unity and completeness of our small family.

I began to spend less time in Cann's. With the advice and help of the consultants, we appointed a new man from outside, a professional retailer, as General Manager. 'This place has no management at all!' the consultant had exclaimed, recommending the move. I had certainly often wondered how it kept going. It might have been losing money, but customers still came in, stock was ordered, a large staff came to work every day, and enough cash flowed to pay their wages. It apparently continued under its own momentum. Habit and loyalty had a lot to do with it. More than once I was told proudly by an elderly woman, 'I've been with the Firm for forty years.' The new Manager didn't face an easy task in this feudal atmosphere.

Aunt Nell didn't take seriously or even bother to read the new organisation charts and job definitions, in which she had been given some such title as Honourable Elder Adviser. When she was in the shop, she continued to be simply the Firm, giving and changing orders, drawing up buying plans with the Secretary, a faithful old employee, and ignoring the General Manager. But she too stayed at home more. She was old and not well, and must sometimes have felt relieved that others were taking over. I didn't expect brilliant things from the new Manager, but I hoped he would stem the losses, and thought that the best way to help was to keep out of his way. I had learned a lot in a few months, and the passion had been gradually seeping out of my involvement with Cann's.

We of the younger generation had grown up with the heady atmosphere that pervades all fashion-dominated milieux. We had also acquired that vanishing trait, pride in a family business. Betty and I had lamented its growing stodginess even more than the diminishing profits. When I accepted the challenge of taking on the reform of the business, I had at first believed I could sweep away the frowst and restore the old atmosphere of glamour and specialness. I had also held equivocal notions about my own role. A few weeks after their investigations began, the head of the consulting firm had suggested to me that I was the obvious person to direct a revival of Cann's. I had objected that I couldn't spend my life that way, but when he replied that it wouldn't take a lifetime, only a few years, I had been tempted, having for a long time harboured a fantasy of myself as a fashion impresario. I had begun to see, though, that I lacked some of the essential talents, and a sufficiently strong commitment. And that, without the flair and singlemindedness my aunts had once brought to it, the business might be restored to profitability, but with an unappealing atmosphere of average ordinariness.

So my objective became the simpler one of safeguarding our share of the family cash, that of myself, my sister and my sister-in-law. There followed discussions with the Tronson family, and with lawyers and accountants, about the future, including drawing up new Articles of Association to avoid the stalemate which the exact division of power between two families presaged. It took a very long time, because Aunt Nell was apt to agree, and then, next day, change her mind.

XIII

Pleasures and Resentments

I now spent more time at Portsea with Erwin and the children. Daniel wasn't yet a playmate for Sarah, and much of the time she ignored him. At Portsea they slept in separate rooms. He didn't sleep much more than she did, but when he was awake he often just sat, solemnly and silently. Not much fun! But she continued to speak of him fondly as 'my baby brother', liked to feed him, and in a photograph taken at Portsea gazes at him lovingly.

Among her favourite books at this time were several by Dare Wright about Edith the Lonely Doll, who longs for a friend, and finds Little Bear, the ideal younger brother, optimistic, courageous and foolish. Sarah greeted with ecstatic laughter every snub and disaster that overtakes Little Bear – when Edith, echoing a grown-up, says, 'You're bad, Little Bear', or when Little Bear, at sea in a stolen boat, falls overboard with a loud splash. Repetition did not diminish her joyous response to these setbacks.

One morning I discovered Daniel sitting on the floor with wet hair plastered to his scalp, and liquid streaming down his face. Sarah, standing abashedly beside him, holding the Flit gun, explained that she had been trying to kill a fly that was buzzing around his head. I could see what a tempting fly fat defenceless Daniel made, sitting bundled up in pale blue orlon, with his legs stuck out in front of him.

As Daniel's infant fragility faded and his span of endurance lengthened, we were no longer confined to the terrace, and I took the children down the zig-zag wooden ramp to the beach. It was a strenuous climb, which in the childless past I had avoided, preferring to drive to the beach by the pier for a swim. Now I descended in a mood of triumphant stoicism, carrying Daniel and a load of towels, buckets, rugs and food, while watching and encouraging Sarah. In one place there was a steep ladder, and here I carried her also, and groped my way down with Sarah clinging to my back, Daniel clasped to my chest, and the gear hung around my neck and arms.

For Sarah the descent was fraught with excitement and terror: the possibility of seeing the fat blue-tongued lizard which lived under the platform at the first turning, and which she had accepted as a 'friendly creature'; the necessity of passing some bloody tufts of rabbit fur caught on the barbed wire – someone had said it must have been killed by a snake, which perhaps was still lying there waiting; and, this danger past, the impetuous rush ahead of us down the last stretch of boards, through the scrub, and onto the beach. It was a calm, protected beach, always deserted. Daniel scrunched his fingers in the sand, Sarah looked for shells at the edge of the water, and I managed to read a few pages, or just stared at the sea and the wide pale sky.

Wherever Sarah went, she was accompanied by one of her collection of stuffed animals – several koalas, a kangaroo, a penguin and a rabbit – which she carried tucked under one arm, as I had carried her when a baby. Once, the rabbit and one of the bears disappeared from outside the house, where she had been watching me root out more pea-plant. We thought they might have been carried off by a frolicsome dog from across the road, and searched the garden there, but we never found them. She accepted a new bear when we went back to town, but Erwin scanned the shops for months, unsuccessfully, for a new rabbit. I looked too, and found one wearing blue velvet trousers, which, priggishly, I didn't buy, remembering a friend's condemnation, years before, of pictures of animals with clothes on, but, foolishly, told Sarah about, so that for weeks she kept demanding the rabbit with blue velvet trousers.

The presence in Sorrento of Dr Edwards was reassuring. He was young, hard-working, rational, and always available; even on Sunday mornings his surgery was crowded. The children saw him often, for minor infections and to complete their schedule of immunisations. One morning, while we were waiting for him to visit the house, Sarah laid an immense poo on the terrace, across the path that lead to the door. Weapon, defensive barricade, placatory offering, love gift, or all of these? Certainly a meaningful gesture.

There was one similar occasion, when, before the astonished and fascinated gaze of her cousin Andy, she deposited another great poo on the carpet in the Bretherton's hall. This time there was no obvious trigger-event, but my guess is that it was defence against my brother-in-law Bruce, who sometimes fixed her with a steely look and a threat of punishment that was not entirely playful. 'Don't let Bruce come up!' she used to say as I was putting her to bed on nights when we were going out.

There were new activities of that winter:

Telephoning in monologue: 'Is that Ossie Burt? I'd like to make an appointment. We are having a meeting at two-thirty. How is Mr Andrew? We are all well thank you.'

Playing sick: A game of role-playing, developed with Barbie, the daughter of friends, older than Sarah, to whom she became passionately attached. It always remained a favourite.

Horse-riding: I don't know how the idea of this perennial little-girl's favourite reached her, but she asked me repeatedly to take her riding. I was quite willing, but didn't know where to find a riding school. We set out several times to search. One cold afternoon we found a railed enclosure, trodden bare and smelling of horses, but closed for the winter. To compensate, she went on a merry-go-round, also about to close, where the boy in charge gave her an extra-long ride and refused payment. Finally we found a stable, also in charge of a young boy, who caught and bridled one of the horses, and sat Sarah on its back while he walked it round the half-cleared paddock. Although insisting that I walk beside her, she had the courage to try, and hung on, even when the horse was urged to a lolloping canter, even when it lowered its head to tear at the grass and she nearly slid down its neck.

We learned how to reach the one place where it was possible to drive down to the ocean beach. You crossed an area of scrub between bay and ocean, which had been surveyed for subdivision during a long-forgotten land boom, and only a sagging wire fence marked the correct sandy track, bumped past a few holiday shacks with faded paint and windows boarded against the winter gales, and climbed a steep rise, where we had to change quickly into low gear. Suddenly the vast untamed ocean lay before us. For me it was always a tremendous moment and I must have exclaimed at it often. Sarah made my exclamation into a ritual feature of the outing. 'Isn't it maaarvellous!' she chanted in mockery, each time we topped the crest.

As the Portsea winter drew to an end, the different species of ti-tree broke one after another into frothy white blossom. Sometimes in the evening we drove through the scrub behind the back beach, where from the tops of the hillocky dunes you could look across a delicately perfumed sea to the pale-blue outline of Mount Martha. Once, Sarah dropped her new plastic sandal out of the car, and perhaps it still lies there, buried in the sand, one of a trail of lost sandals, hers and Daniel's, strewn around the world.

Fortunate days in idyllic places, the happiest I have known. But also a strenuous and disciplined life. Even with part-time help, looking after young children demands immense energy and constant attention. Whatever else you manage to do, you remain ceaselessly aware of them, always ready to drop everything else for some ministration of comfort or love. In this intense involvement, old habits and passions are discarded wholesale. And by me. mostly without struggle or regret. 'The basic attitude of mothers is resentment,' I read recently, and it might seem a modern platitude, but it was not so for me.

Yet resentment occasionally welled up. Not against the children. I was rarely even mildly irritated by them. When things got too much, instead of yelling at the children, I lashed out at Erwin: 'Selfish. . . self-centred. . . don't know what it means to share equally. . . can't see how unfair. . .', until in a blind rage I slammed out of the house and started up the car, half-convinced that I would drive on and on and never go back. At Portsea I drove, in fact, to a stretch of ocean front further away than we usually went, where bulldozers had laid bare an eroding clay slope on which a few ugly houses squatted in the drizzling rain, facing a flat and melancholy sea. (It wasn't only on days of happiness that nature echoed my moods.) Into this desolation I yelled my grievances, tears streaming down my face, until, exhausted and feeling ridiculous, I turned and drove home.

At the end of winter, I caught a throat infection. Some forgotten crisis, and fear of being thought a malingerer, made me go on working, and by the time I reached Portsea at the end of the week, I felt very ill. Dr Edwards diagnosed pneumonia, and I retired to bed, but after a couple of days, out of compunction at leaving Erwin to cope with the children and the house, I got up and went shopping in Sorrento. My temperature shot up again, and this time I was ordered to stay in bed for three weeks. Through the doctor and the Sorrento fish shop, Erwin met Lynne, a cheerful girl who was willing to come every day and help with the children. I moved to my mother's bed overlooking the sun-flecked terrace and the water gleaming through the ti-tree, and read solidly, as I hadn't done since Daniel's birth. The children, who had avoided me when I was feverish and passive, crawled and scuffled on the bed. 'Poor Mummy!' Lynne said.

Tantrums and illnesses make splendid breaks in the domestic round, but they shouldn't become habitual, and with us they did not. Instead, we took to a sort of vagabondage, wandering off in the car to explore the Victorian countryside, taking the children with us, but giving ourselves a taste of freedom and the stimulus of new sights.

We set off for the first time in late spring, when I had recovered , and Daniel was at the age Sarah had been when we first took her to France. We had given the Daimler back to my father when it had become apparent that our stay would be a long one, and now had a car of our own, a Holden station wagon, second-hand, pig-pink, and larger than any car we would have driven in England. It could be made into a snug travelling home for the children. On this first journey, Sarah occupied the back seat, made into a platform by building up the floor with luggage, filling the dip at the back of the seat with packets of nappies, and covering the lot with a brown rug stretched tight. The sides were padded with rolled blankets, and she had toys and books for waking hours, and rugs for sleep. Daniel lay in the wicker basket in the back compartment, wedged in place by suitcases and picnic gear. Installed like this, they remained cheerful and uncomplaining for hours at a time.

We left Portsea after lunch, cross-country, by way of Tooradin and Koo-wee-rup to the Prince's Highway, and then, while I read to the children *The Four Billygoats Gruff*, through a string of small townships spread out in the evening light, to our chosen motel. We stopped in motels, the new alternative to the beer-smelling family hotels which had previously supplied reluctant accommodation to travellers. They were usually just outside a township, looking onto paddocks or the fresh-smelling bush, enclosed in profound Australian country silence. There would be a family room big enough for the four of us, and in the morning, a generous breakfast pushed through a hatch. We picnicked in a jumble of bedclothes, trays, dish-covers and warm children's bodies. Sarah and Daniel were happy to be constantly with us, and for me, the feeding and washing and nappy-changing took on the charm of improvisation. Our first motel was the best of all, with a huge window facing across empty ochre paddocks to a line of hills. After breakfast, Sarah shepherded Daniel out into the sun, found a swing, helped him to clamber on, and pushed it gently, watched by a pet magpie.

We went shopping on Saturday morning in the main street of Sale, crowded with shoppers and lined with station wagons. We couldn't explore its quiet grassy side streets, because Daniel was too heavy to carry, so we got back into the car and drove off towards the Strezlecki Ranges. Years before, the hills had been cleared for dairying, but now they were overgrown with bracken and sassafras, and studded with the fretted trunks of burnt gums. We stopped often for Erwin to take photographs. I moved the car gently, so as not to wake the sleeping children, and between moves walked along the road, relishing the clean fragrant air. The hillsides were hatched with cow paths, but we saw neither man nor beast. At the crest of the range there had once been a farm, its site marked by greener grass, a clump of laurels, and a dark row of pines, though only a chimney remained of the house. We continued down to a forlorn little harbour, with a pier built out over deep milky-green water, once the link to the city for those farmers on the hilltop.

Next day we turned north, through lonely country with no houses for miles, and picnicked beside a clear river, where the children played in the shallows. In the mountain township of Omeo, we are told at the hotel, 'Lucky to get in! Its Show Day tomorrow.' They give us two drab rooms and dinner in the deserted dining-room, while the boom of male voices resounds from the bar. I am pleased about the Show. Growing up in Australia as a city child, I absorbed, from books and occasional country visits, a romantic vision of bush life, from which I felt wistfully excluded. The Show will be a compensating gift for Sarah. In the morning we go up to the showground, on a hill outside the town. Early in the day, it has the atmosphere of a family party, with much greeting and kissing. Men with notebooks inspect a few pens of sheep and cattle, and ladies in white hats set out jars of jam and sponge cakes on trestle tables. We sit in the shade of some pines, the only spectators to watch half a dozen little girls manoeuvre their ponies in the ring. But Sarah, who hasn't absorbed all those girls' stories about the outback, is soon restive, so we leave.

A little way beyond the town, a faded sign nailed to a tree announces 'Camping Area', and we turn onto a track which winds through scattered trees, resembling the park of an English country house, but dry, bleached, and already shimmering in the heat. We stop for a picnic lunch in a small patch of shade under a she-oak, above a gully crossed by a flat wooden bridge. I feel at home in this parched aromatic silent country, but the sun is too strong for Daniel, the heat, already in November, is stupefying, and we don't let Sarah play by the creek for fear of snakes.

So we return to the car and climb into cooler air. Over the crest, the road is steeper and the forest more lush; immense trees with creamy trunks soar upwards and plunge downwards, dappled sunlight glinting through their narrow leaves. Then the gentle open valley and a good home-cooked meal, served by the new-migrant owners of the motel.

There were more such days, and other trips, from which we returned home dazzled by infinite variations of light and colour, our equanimity restored by space and silence.

XIV

Another move

That summer, the family party assembled at Portsea was smaller, and we were keenly aware of the absence of my mother and my brother, Bruce. Even so, at weekends the house was crowded. Mrs Ramplin had left, and Betty and I did the shopping and cooked enormous meals. No-one seemed to feel anything but relief that this would be the last time we would be all there together. We had agreed that the house, shared unmanageably between three families, should be sold, and there was already an auctioneer's placard by the gate.

When everyone went home in February, we went too, and installed ourselves in my mother's flat in the front of the Power Street house, where we remained for six months. In retrospect, they seem the least luminous period of my life with Sarah, and that was perhaps in part due to the flat itself, the home of old people without energy to see that it was repaired or cleaned. We shared it with my father, and the rooms available to us were cramped and gloomy. The parched garden outside sloped down to a gate left permanently open onto a busy street, so we could not leave the children there to play. I missed the shining tranquillity of the sea. The work in Cann's took up less time, but it had lost its initial excitement, and I now had to keep house as well. I still hoped for an early agreement on the future of the business, and chafed at the continuing delays. We began to see old friends, but not often; it happened that the two couples closest to us were in England that year. And my vital spirits still belonged with the children. Daniel was in his second year, the age that requires the most unrelenting attention. For Sarah he was not yet a constantly rewarding or available playmate. Sarah herself, as winter approached, was often whiny and discontented.

I surmised that she was going through one of those recurrent periods when all the possibilities of one stage have been explored, and she was waiting to burst through to the next. Perhaps the play and rituals of the nursery school had become too tame, and she needed more stimulating schooling. I decided to send her to Mountvale, a progressive school favoured by academic parents.

The activities at Mountvale turned out to be much the same as at the Robert Cochrane: toys, puzzles, painting, modelling in clay, a lot of clambering and running about outside, sometimes a story or a song. The difference was that there was no regular programme, and that the teachers made no attempt to suggest, encourage or invite the children to do anything. No-one at Mountvale made any gesture of welcome to Sarah, and she spent most of her time sitting alone on the outside steps, looking wistfully across the playground. Most mornings, I sat with her for half an hour or so. After several weeks, I called in at the Robert Cochrane. Yes, they had kept her place and would be happy to welcome her back.

I never had trouble finding someone to look after the children in the daytime. After our initial luck with Janny, who had meanwhile had her baby, I found that the best way was to advertise in *The Age*. There was always a large number of replies. Sometimes I took the first person to turn up; sometimes I determined to see everyone and then didn't know how to decide. But I only made one, short-lived, mistake. The others were all competent in the house, easy to get on with, and pleasant with the children. Each stayed for about three months and then left, for a reason I had known about from the start, to get married, to have a baby, or to go to Europe. For them it was a fill-in job of a kind not easy to find. All in all, the nurses and I were useful to each other, and we got on happily. One reason was that they didn't live in. Friday nights were lightened by the knowledge that we had two whole days to ourselves; doubtless they felt the same.

Our first nurse in the front flat was Fat Robin, so called to distinguish her from a later very skinny Robin. She read Sarah the *Just So Stories*, and *The Jungle Book*, taught her the alphabet, and gave her a box of coloured felt pens. Her successor was a wiry elderly lady who asked us to call her Margot, and who had worked since she was thirteen as nursery maid, nanny and housekeeper in England, before coming to Australia. In a cheerful impervious way she dealt firmly with everything, from the children's meals to overseeing their farewells on the rare occasions when we went out at night. A boss, in fact! She was the only one of the nurses who would have stayed indefinitely, but on her way home one night she was injured by a runaway car while she waited at a bus stop. When Sarah and I visited her in hospital, she seemed cheerfully indestructible, demonstrating how her thick overcoat had saved her life and explaining the intricacies of her compensation claim. Later, we went to see her at home, and she gave Sarah a little pearl and silver necklace, part of the jetsam of mementoes accumulated in a life spent helping others.

The best times of autumn and winter were again our escapes to the country. The station wagon was now set up differently, to make a large padded playground for two, the 'snoo-nest'. But the penalty for taking too long to write a book is that values change. I am now so aware of the need to fasten children into well-designed car seats, that the memory of the snoo-nest is occasionally overlaid with a sense of criminal fecklessness. More often, I think of this padded refuge, with the two children playing together or lying asleep, as an emblem of our happiness.

Sarah helped to prepare the snoo-nest, carrying things out to the car, and making sure that Daniel's bears and tractors were not left behind. The children could stay in the car for hours without becoming restless or quarrelsome. They played with their toys, or chattered to each other, their heads close together. They were not interested in watching the countryside, although Sarah liked to see animals, a horse, or a string of cows going home at milking-time. 'There they go, one after the other,' she would say, in a phrase that remained a favourite. When the children were tired, they fell asleep. Long after they both stopped taking a morning nap, they would drop off in the car an hour or so after setting out. Sometimes, if

Daniel went to sleep first, Sarah would complain, 'The boy's taking up all the room!' not resentfully, but in a caricature of superiority.

More than once, when we stopped in the country, Erwin and I looked down at the two children lying asleep, with flushed faces and bodies sprawled against each other, and shared our astonished gratitude that there could be such children, that we could be their parents.

We stopped often, and each time I put on the children's shoes and socks, which they always kicked off in the car. Four socks, entangled with the toys or pushed down the back of the seat, to be found, turned right side out, and pulled on; four brown lace-up shoes to be located, laces unknotted, shoes pushed onto limp feet, tongues straightened and laces tied in a bow and then in a knot; as many as thirty uncooperative feet to be shod in the course of the day.

During the outings of the winter, Sarah and Daniel invented country pleasures of their own, different from ours but compatible with them. Walking along a deserted road early one morning, (away from the highways all roads were deserted), we came to a river, which let in a gash of sunlight between dark walls of forest. On the bridge Daniel suddenly discovered the eternal pastime of throwing stones into water. The first one curved upward and fell with a plop and a splash; both children laughed and raced to the roadside for more stones, and back to toss them over the wooden parapet.

Beyond Bendigo, in thinly timbered grazing country, they played beside a large puddle left by the winter rains in the middle of a clay track, launching boats of leaves and sticks, scooping up the soft mud with picnic spoons, and pouring water from one plastic cup to another.

Near Healesville, the smooth white branch of a fallen gum became, first, a jetty from which they fished, and then a horse which they rode astride, while Erwin bounced it to give them a springy gallop.

At Christmas Hills, among the debris of a burned-down house, Sarah found two baking tins, and then discovered that the brick chimney, the only part of the house left standing, held an iron cooking stove with an oven door that still opened. They played at being cooks for nearly an hour, filling dishes with rubble and running to the oven to bake them.

Near Woori Yallock, one sombre day with a sharp wind blowing, we drove around looking for a sheltered picturesque place to picnic, and finally gave up, and stopped beside the road, in straggly bush. I forget what game they played that day, but I remember looking down at the yellow clay, the small sharp-sided stones, and the few shallow puddles, and marvelling at the small means with which they could create an absorbing world.

We went to the Wildlife Sanctuary at Healesville, where the largest animals rove freely – emus, rather shabby and moulting, which greet you at the gate with throaty squawks, and kangaroos, which took Sarah's banana skins in their long rubbery fingers, and ate them appreciatively. She stroked them, put her face against their fur, and announced that she wanted to sleep in their shelter. 'They might push against you, or roll on you,' Erwin warned. 'I wouldn't mind. I'd push against them too.' 'They might pee on you.' Sarah's face showed what a gleeful thought that was.

In September, we went to Sydney for a longer holiday. We stayed in a motel at King's Cross, tucked away from noise and traffic, where we had two connecting rooms and a small pantry. We ate all our meals there, bought in local shops or ordered from the restaurant. Sydney friends came to visit us; Sarah and Daniel allowed themselves to be put to bed in one room, while we ate and drank and talked in the other. We hadn't had such a sociable time for years.

In the daytime, we took it in turns to go off separately. Or rather, Erwin went off several times to visit galleries and gallery directors, and I had one day of freedom, while he took the children to the zoo. I put on a navy linen suit which I didn't wear with them because it would be filthy in no time (what Sarah identified as 'town clothes'), and had lunch with an eminent barrister whom I'd known during the war, when we had worked for the same boss. I'd been rather in awe of him then, and there was an uncharacteristic bravado about my ringing him. Our former chief had recently died, and we talked about the book of reminiscences that had recently been published, and about the possibility that I might write his biography. Nothing was being put to immediate test, but even to discuss a role outside family life was exhilarating. I had another chance in Canberra on the way home, lunching at the University without the children, where I met a sociologist I had known in New York, heard the latest professional gossip, found I could still contribute an aphoristic comment, and enjoyed pretending for a little while that I still belonged to the academic world.

Thinking about these occasions, I feel the lack of a myth to represent women's submergence in maternity and slow re-emergence. This phenomenon of our times is so different from anything in the past that the old stories can't be stretched to fit. Lacking a myth, I am repeatedly reminded, now that Daniel has left school, of the similarity of a woman's years of child-indenture to a man's time in the army. Wartime, not military service. If it doesn't kill you, it'll make a man of you! One emerges at last from the relentless discipline, immensely thankful for the experience, and thankful also never to have to go through it again. The few hours in Sydney were not the end of child service but for both of us (Erwin changed fewer nappies, but he gave himself generously to the duties of fatherhood), they were a reminder of the glitter of civilian life.

Our time in Sydney wasn't always rewarding. Some of my attempts to keep the children occupied and cheerful without the resources of home merely resulted in exhaustion and boredom. I walked with them along the road skirting the Rushcutters' Bay Oval, hoping to reach the water and show them the boats, but the distance seemed endless, with nothing to look at but close-mown grass on one side, and brick villas with drawn blinds on the other. I turned back before we got half way. Daniel was so exasperatingly slow. I never went for walks with them at home. That night, when the children had gone to bed, resentment once more brimmed over, and I hurled accusations at Erwin, and flounced out, to stride down sleazy sodium-flared Darlinghurst Road, yelling and muttering to myself, until self-pity flickered out in exhaustion.

On our way home, heading towards Canberra, where we were to stay with friends, we came to Goulburn, 'City of Lilacs', as a hoarding at the entrance to the town announced. In the City of Lilacs, in limpid silence, beside a row of cottages glowing in the evening light, the children tumbled from the car and ran along a grassy road, and we all recovered from the heat and confinement of the drive. There was still a long way to go, and we suddenly decided to have dinner in a restaurant before continuing. The meal alone together, the four of us, in a place where no-one knew us, and no-one knew where we were, had the enchantment of a stolen lovers' meeting.

When we got back to Melbourne, I learned that in my absence Aunt Nell had called a board meeting and carried a resolution terminating my salary. I went to see the Chairman, who shrugged apologetically. 'There was nothing I could do. Your Aunt is a very determined woman.' He didn't suggest there was anything I could do either, but when I asked if the meeting had been constitutional, since I hadn't received notice of it, he admitted that it had not. So the next time our amateur board gathered in Aunt Nell's office, I moved that the proceedings of the last meeting be declared invalid. Aunt Nell must have been tipped off by the Chairman with another look of helplessness, for she said nothing, and did not move her resolution a second time.

We met less frequently from then on. Aunt Nell's health was failing and often she did not come into the shop for weeks at a stretch. The last time I saw her, two years later, shortly before her death, every trace of hostility between us had vanished, and she showed me the same affectionate sympathy as in the distant past.

XV

The Day's Round

We returned from Sydney to another new home. Betty and her family had moved into the house they had built after my mother's death, and we took over the flat at the back of the Power Street house. Recognising that we must remain in Melbourne for some time to come, we invited my mother-in-law, Müttchen, to fly out from London. The new flat was large, convenient and secluded, and it opened onto a garden where the children could play safely. After eighteen months of improvisation, we had a home which felt like our own.

In the children's new bedroom upstairs, next to ours, Sarah slept in a bed in a recessed corner, Daniel in a drop-sided cot against the opposite wall. So that they wouldn't be woken early by the sun, Erwin made wooden shutters for the east-facing windows. Sarah woke up between half-past seven and eight, and came into our room, where often I was still asleep, though Erwin had usually been up for some time. She woke me, but if I said I wanted to sleep a little longer, she left unprotestingly and went downstairs to find Erwin. Together they collected the milk and newspapers from the front gate. Sometimes, in that rambling house, which had seven doors to the garden, she missed him; then, when they met, she would ask, 'with a lover's yearning', Erwin said, 'Where were you? I was looking for you.'

They had breakfast together. Erwin made tea for himself and a drink for her, at first milky tea, but later he persuaded her to have chocolate milk. 'I'll prepare it for you!' She had toast and vegemite, which she liked him to cut into little squares. 'We're having a little party,' she would say. Or, because he made a ceremony of preparing it, she ate an egg. She wanted to put it into the boiling water herself, but she was clumsy and likely to crack it, so Erwin held her hand; then they ate the egg together in alternate spoonfuls. Or Sarah played at being a baby, asking to be fed.

She began to invent a style of badinage which particularly appealed to him. She would say impatiently, when the bread was already in the toaster, 'I want a toast!' and when he asked 'What am I doing?' reply, 'Not giving me any toast!' or later, more inventively, 'Catching a crocodile!' Or 'Fishing for a shark.' While the memory of such interchanges was still vivid, I wrote:

'I search for words to characterise her play-acting with Erwin, using hand gestures and exaggerated facial expressions. Amused, satirical, detached, gentle. Making fun of her own impatience, and perhaps of a world where desires couldn't be instantly gratified, even by a loving and attentive father.'

Often her last words to Erwin at night were, 'See you in the morning when we have breakfast together.' But she was not jealously possessive, like someone not sure of their love. She liked Daniel and me to be there too. If Daniel was awake, but I wanted to sleep a little longer, she shepherded him downstairs, and they played together until Erwin called them to breakfast. Erwin wondered how Daniel got out of the high-sided cot. 'I'll show you,' said Sarah. 'Come on, Daniel!' He stood up in the cot, and she pulled and tugged him until he toppled head-first over the gate, and thumped onto the floor. They both grinned proudly.

If I was awake and ready to get up, she waited for me, and we descended the narrow staircase in an awkward slow procession. Both the children wanted to hold my hand, but we also had to carry a basket with Daniel's bears and tractors, and they each wanted a whole hand, not one shared with the bear-basket. Sometimes the solution was to leave Daniel at the top of the stairs while I escorted Sarah down, and then return for him; but he didn't like being left behind, and usually we all came down together, clumsily, shuffling sideways. No-one watched our entry into the day, but it was one of the times when I was most conscious of pride in my two handsome loving children, and in being their trusted guardian.

If Erwin was still in bed when the children woke up, they got into bed with us, Sarah with Erwin and Daniel with me. Daniel sat on my knees, hammered cheerfully with his fists, kicked, bounced and giggled; but Sarah lay close to Erwin, warm and still as a peach in a summer orchard.

Sometimes Erwin and Sarah brought me breakfast in bed. Sarah stayed while I ate, and amused herself trying on my clothes. A blouse was long enough to make her a dress; she tottered around on high heels, ready to go to town;

once, she put on my long dark blue mohair dressing-gown. She asked me to tie the girdle, and then looked at herself in the mirror, her head high and the long, straight robe falling in folds around her feet. 'Do I look like a Queen?' she asked.

At half-past eight the nurse arrived. We had two nurses while we lived in the back flat, Thin Robin and Beverly. Both were young; they seemed barely out of school, although both were engaged to be married. Thin Robin was tall and gangly, and often looked anxious, though she responded to the children's gaiety. 'I never knew children could have so much freedom and yet be so marvellous,' she said.

Beverly was small, with a childish round face and fair hair, a pale version of Sarah. They looked like sisters. After lunch, when Beverly did the ironing while Daniel slept, a continuous babble of voices and laughter reached us from the laundry. For Sarah's birthday, Beverly made a present to satisfy a longing only a contemporary would have known about, a white petticoat frilled with broderie anglaise and threaded with yellow ribbon.

Robin lived nearby, and Sarah took to going down to the gate to watch for her appearance at the end of the street. Daniel often went too, and they stood had-in-hand in their dressing gowns while the rush hour traffic streamed past. If Robin arrived while we were still at breakfast, Sarah was overwhelmed with disappointment. 'I wanted to wait for you,' she told her, in tears. Robin helped to dress the children and get Sarah ready for school.

Daniel was the devil to dress, wriggling and squirming, and making it almost impossible to get his clothes on. I forced myself to remain equable, as I had always been with Sarah, until one day I got fed-up and pushed him roughly down on his back, holding him tightly enough to hurt while I dragged on his trousers and pullover. To my surprise, instead of crying, he giggled in obvious delight. I told Robin. 'Yes,' she said. 'The other day I was struggling with him as usual, and he looked at me, very pleased with himself, and said, "We fighting!"' She looked pleased too, smiling as she imitated his voice.

Before Sarah was born, I used to think, with Simone de Beauvoir, that differences in attitudes and social behaviour between the sexes were entirely due to social conditioning. Watching them grow changed my personal conviction, and now it seems obvious to me that the innate differences are vast. Sarah was always sociable and interested in knowing about people; Daniel was from the start self-contained and technically-minded.

While Sarah was at school, I left Daniel in charge of the nurse and, since I seldom now needed to go into town, I settled down at my desk in the upstairs glassed-in sleep-out, to read and write. I had taken up again one of the sociological projects I had been working on before Sarah was born. The house, like a medieval manor or a village, could shelter a number of small worlds, each going about its business without disturbing the others. I worked on my balcony, looking out over a sea of tree tops islanded by the gables of left-over Victorian outbuildings. Downstairs, Müttchen dressed herself and ate a leisurely breakfast in her room opening onto the garden. Erwin withdrew to his studio in the front of the house. Grandpa reigned in the enormous front dining-room, from which he came and went on errands of his own. Robin and the children had to themselves kitchen, playroom, laundry and garden. I seldom heard them from my balcony, but Erwin said that at lunchtime their laughter reached his studio.

Sometimes when Sarah returned from school, she came upstairs to look for me. Once, I didn't hear her until, suddenly, she parted the curtain between my balcony and the bedroom, and I saw her eager glowing face beside me. An irritable shadow must have crossed my face. 'I won't stay long,' she said, in a tone of love and concern. 'I only came to say hullo, and then I'm going down to have lunch with Beverly.'

She never did say long on these visits. She would ask if I were going to town, and remind me not to leave without saying goodbye, then go down to the kitchen, where Robin or Beverly prepared lunch for the children and Mama. At first she sometimes returned with complaints. 'Robin's making me eat soup,' or 'Robin won't give me a biscuit.' 'Well that's between you and Robin. You'll have to sort it out together,' I told her. If I were going to the office for lunch, I went down to the kitchen to say goodbye, and she put her arms around my neck, and her warm buttery crumby cheek against mine.

In the back flat, Sarah and Daniel learned to play together. They now had their own indoor territory, the playroom, and a big garden behind the house away from the dangers of the street. I felt the burden of constant attention suddenly become lighter. Someone's attention; thanks to Robin and Beverly, it wasn't always mine, but they were not there in the evenings or at weekends, nor for two months in the summer. One day in the office, while we were assembling for a Board meeting, someone asked me how the children were. 'Fine!' I replied. 'They've reached the age when I don't have to worry about them any more.' The Board members, all experienced parents, laughed indulgently.

The children had small green tricycles, with red handlebars decorated with streamers that fluttered in the wind. They pedalled round and round the drive that circled the back garden, slowly uphill, while they gazed about with a solemn and superior air, and then furiously downhill, laughing and egging each other on.

Beverly taught them the game of rhinoceroses. It was a very simple game. They each broke two large thorns from a rose bush and stuck them with spit to their noses and foreheads, then came to present themselves to me. The comparison of their rose-petal faces balancing the delicately-curved thorns with a thick-skinned, muddy, suspicious animal was ludicrous, and yet there was something rhinoceros-like, in the way they thrust their heads forward, in their innocence (real), and their belligerence (pretended).

Sarah invited guests of her own for the first time. It was her suggestion, and she gave me the names of the school friends she wanted to ask, of whom two could come on the chosen day. I had never waited more nervously for a party to begin. I even put a cloth on the table in the garden, before laying out the milk and wholemeal biscuits. But I needn't have worried. The children were absorbed in their own activities from the moment they arrived until their mothers came to take them home. Daniel enjoyed himself hugely, leaping and pirouetting and giggling in front of the visitors while they had tea. Later, I saw three excited squealing four-year-old girls racing across the grass, calling to each other, 'He's coming, he's coming! Quick, don't let him catch you! Hide!' while behind them, waving a leafy wand, pranced two-year-old Daniel.

When the school year began again in February, we decided to send Sarah to the local State School. In spite of the fiasco of Mountvale, I was still impatient for her to learn more, and specifically to learn to read. Not in order to give her a start in the rat-race, nor so that I could congratulate myself on her precocity, but because she would relish the tension of effort and the triumph of achievement. I telephoned the school before term started, hoping to discuss whether it was a good idea to send her, but was told that none of the staff would be there until the first day of term. So at nine-o'clock on the first day, holding her hand, I went through the little back gate and crossed the asphalt playground.

We waited in a big bare hall with a crowd of mothers and new pupils, while the older children filed into their classrooms matter-of-factly, as if there had been no long summer holiday. When the hall was nearly empty, the headmistress appeared, not to welcome us to the school, but merely to give instructions, about towels, sandshoes and shoe-bags, all to be clearly marked with the child's name, five shillings to be paid for drawing materials, and the children to line up at five to nine on the west side of the playground, unless it was raining. We were sent away until next day. At home, I found a shoe-bag which I had made in the needlework class at my own school, chose a pretty turquoise hand-towel, and lettered Sarah's name on the bottom of the little basket Theo had given her. The dour reception had not extinguished my optimism.

A year later, recalling that day, I wrote:

The new school year brings reminders of last year, when I took Sarah to Manningtree Road. How I loved to act as her guide to new reaches of the world, to accompany her on that first day, and wait with her and all the other mothers of young ones starting school. Pride in my beautiful lively Sarah, joyful anticipation of the world of learning which she was entering, protectiveness. I used to feel that I had created the world so that I might lay it at her feet, whatever was good, and that I stood as a shield between her and evil, to guard her from cruelty, deceit, rebuff, and tedious warping schools.

The next morning, we were shown her classroom. It was small and crammed with desks, and the windows were too high to see out of. The five-year-olds, we were told, would spend their time much as in nursery school. But there was no space for them to move about, their voices must be kept low so as not to disturb children in adjoining rooms, and they would be allowed outside only at mid-morning recess and lunchtime.

Farewells to mothers were expected to be brief, and to

my astonishment, so they were. Without a chirp of protest or anguish, all those children, on the first school-day of their lives, had suddenly disappeared into the classroom and their mothers had gone. I was the only one left. The teacher held Sarah, while I, too, compliantly fled.

I went to see the headmistress, a thin grey woman who had learned, in a lifetime of teaching, to treat children and parents with bright no-nonsense firmness. There were no formal reading lessons in the first year, she said, but they did begin Preparation for Reading. Objects in the classroom were labelled with their names: Chair, Table, Blackboard. One day, a child would say, 'Look, that word begins with the same letter as my name!' Other children would begin to study the printed labels, and together they would start to learn the alphabet for themselves. I didn't believe a word of it, and besides Sarah more or less knew the alphabet already. I was immensely disappointed, but not yet ready to give up.

School started at nine and continued until half past three, and the children took sandwiches for lunch. I thought this would at first be too long for Sarah to be among strangers, so I arranged for her to come home for lunch. Twice I collected her from the classroom at the end of the morning. On the third day, I told her that I would wait at the gate, showed her exactly where I would be, and was there before the bell rang, but she did not appear. I found her sitting on the classroom floor, surrounded by her silent classmates bent over their grease-proof-wrapped lunches, while the teacher watched them from a chair. Sarah looked up without speaking; she seemed frightened, and her mouth was full of someone else's sandwich. Her stricken look decided me; we went home and never returned, not even to collect the shoe-bag and the turquoise towel. I rang the Robert Cochrane and learned that they were still holding her place. Once more, thankfully, we returned there.

The Robert Cochrane was five minutes away by car, and we arranged to share the driving with the Boddingtons, who lived opposite and whose eldest son, Jamie, was in Sarah's class. Sarah was always a bit apprehensive about going in someone else's car. If the Bods took her to school, she pleaded urgently for one of us, Erwin or me or Grandpa, to collect her at lunchtime, but usually I did the morning run. Daniel often came with us and sometimes Jamie's younger brother Alastair.

I loved driving the carload of children through the quiet streets in the fresh morning, past leafy gardens and cottages with ornate cast-iron verandahs. Sarah recited the names of the streets: 'Power Street, Riversdale Road, Belgrave Street, Thomas Street, Auburn Road, Hepburn Street, Minona Street.' The school was tucked away at the bottom of dead-end Minona Street, in what had been part of the garden of an imposing Victorian mansion, whose creamy façade could be glimpsed between the remaining trees. The one-storey school building was airy and secluded but accessible; parents and brothers and sisters could come and go easily.

When we arrived, Jamie hopped out and disappeared into the crowd of children; Alastair and Daniel walked slowly, holding my hands, and Sarah stayed with us, so that we reached the classroom as a cheerful convoy. 'You bring quite a crowd these days,' Miss Auchterlonie said. She was the head teacher and Sarah was in her class that year, the senior class, in the largest room, where in winter a fire burned behind a wire guard. Often I stayed for ten minutes and Sarah took charge of Daniel. 'Come on Daniel, I want to show you Dollies' Corner.' 'Stay a little longer,' she sometimes asked when I was ready to leave, and if I could I did; though if I said, 'No, I really must go,' she allowed me to leave without fuss. Often she called out a last command: 'Fish fingers for lunch!' – because they were 'my favourite', but also because she wanted to display the love and attention she commanded at home.

She told the teachers long stories about happenings at home and family outings, Miss Auchterlonie told me, but at home she didn't talk about school, though she liked to sing us their songs, with heavy emphasis and a hint of mystery – 'Ten little gentlemen standing in a row. Bow down gentlemen, bow down low.'

We were lucky, I know now, to find and be accepted by this school, with its pleasant teachers, bright well-equipped building, and familial atmosphere. At that time, though, I didn't recognise my good fortune, not having yet learned how far below my vague but exalted ideal every school falls, nor how impossible it is to make an informed choice, since you don't learn much about a school until your child goes there, and then it's too late. The notes I made later about the Robert Cochrane, which had twice welcomed me back, were disparaging: A very dead atmosphere. The other children looked dull little puddings who didn't much notice what went on. Those terrible discussion sessions, when the teacher was reluctant to tell the children anything, trying desperately to get them to volunteer, and then offered, not information, but homily – you must clean your teeth, and eat plenty of fruit and vegetables.

But I concluded with resigned acceptance: This year Sarah seemed happier at kindergarten, and I came to think that if it offered nothing very positive (though it did give the companionship of other children), it didn't pose any great threat either.

XVI

Occasions

Robin and I took the children to the Show – the Royal Melbourne Agricultural Show, held annually on a permanent site in the desolate western suburbs. The Show had been one of the few recurring events of my childhood that I had always enjoyed, and I was impatient to share its pleasures with them – the sleek cattle in their straw-smelling pens, the curly-horned rams, the axemen flailing their arms in a cloud of flying chips, the thick column of yellow water perpetually gushing from a Danks' pump, the doll-size samples of Weeties and Rosella Sauce and Sunblest Raisins. The show revealed an abundance and energy totally unlike everyday glimpses of boring adult life.

I was too impatient. The teeming variety was far beyond the capacity of Sarah, four and a half, and Daniel, little more than two. It seemed we had hardly found a parking space, and walked miles to the entrance turnstiles, before I had to suggest to Robin that it was time to go home. Standing with flushed face and untidy hair, holding Daniel in her arms, jostled by the crowd, she agreed. Still, Sarah had been lifted up to stroke the noses of a good many horses, and Daniel's confidence that the world would meet his desires had been strengthened. 'What are you going to see at the Show, Dan?' Betty had asked. 'Elephants!' said Daniel, who just then was infatuated with those beasts. 'Don't be silly Dan, there aren't any elephants at the Show.' But he did see elephants, three different kinds, toy elephants on sticks among the beribboned kewpies, a drawing of an elephant on a poster, and a plywood pie stall shaped like an elephant, with a window in its side from which we bought pies for lunch.

The Nursery School term ended with a Christmas party. Sarah had been dropping hints about surprises in store. At table, she sang in her monotonous voice a monotonous new song, 'We wish you a Merry Christmas, we wish you a Merry Christmas, we wish you a Merry Christmas, and a Happy New Year.' The morning of the party was hot and clear. While I tied the pink sash of her best dress, Sarah hopped up and down with pleasure at the thought of showing it off. However she had no chance for that, because when we got to school, she was whisked away to get ready for her part in the nativity play. Sarah wasn't Mary or Joseph or even an angel, but one of the crowd of silent witnesses, a sheep, with her party dress hidden under a fleece of stiff white paper. She stood with the ox and the ass among her fellow sheep, giving little glances to the side to make sure she was in the right place, but not looking at me, gravely absorbed in the performance, her brown eyes shining. And never was little lamb more adored by her big sheep mother, perched precariously on a tiny kindergarten chair.

After the play there was tea for the mums and cakes and sweets for the children. Sarah said goodbye to an elderly Austrian woman, who told me that her appointment was not being renewed because her qualifications were not regarded as adequate. She hugged Sarah lovingly, as I had often seen her do on other mornings, behaviour not included in the training of the self-possessed younger teachers. I resolved to send the school committee a letter of protest, and never did.

I took Sarah and Müttchen to the pantomime. When Erwin and I had gone to the theatre during the winter, she had quizzed us about what went on there, and hearing mention of the pantomime, she begged to go. I was eager too; it was another rectification of my past. I had never been taken as a child, but had listened wistfully to the enthusiastic reports of my cousins. The pantomime was on only in the mornings, and a fierce January sun beat down on the parking lot, but once we had adjusted to the dark, the theatre revealed a shabby gilt-and-red-velvet grandeur. The show was The Wizard of Oz, and I don't know what Sarah made of it. She wasn't bored, since she sat quite still, with the same look of wide-eyed absorption as at the nursery school play, and in the interval, self-possessed and curious, went to the Ladies (and somehow managed to lose her necklace). But she didn't call out with other children when invited to, and afterwards she asked no questions and made no comment.

We drove sixty miles to Point Lonsdale, to visit our friends Camo and Ann. Sarah spent most of the day with their much older daughters, walking down to the beach with them well ahead of Daniel and me. We sat for a long time over supper, because I enjoyed presenting the family business as satirical farce. So it was dark when we got into the car to drive home. 'Will the children be alright?' Camo asked. He looked at them sitting side by side in the padded snoo-nest, holding a blanket up to their chins, their faces bright with identical show-off grins, and said, 'I can see they will be.' Some occasions when Sarah slept in the car signify to me missed experiences: the geese in France, and a detour through a bird sanctuary taken to break the monotony of a long Australian drive. The unseen geese and the missed birds are gaps that can never be filled, but sleep that night was a positive achievement, proof of their competence in living, and I was reassuringly aware of it all the way home.

In the late afternoon, Sarah sometimes watched television with Grandpa, and she began to acquire the rudiments of modern culture, learning who the Beatles were, and Ron Barassi, the dark handsome captain of Carlton, Grandpa's football team. But her favourite programme was *The Happy Show*, a daily children's programme on a commercial channel. I loved it too, because of the rows of lively children's faces, which the camera scanned between the corny jokes and the advertisements. Sarah asked if she could go, and I applied for tickets. She looked forward to it eagerly, asking for weeks beforehand, 'When are we going to the Happy Show?' Everyone at school knew about it.

When the day finally arrived, after lunch, and before I took her upstairs to put on her best dress, I suggested that she rest for a while. She no longer had a regular nap, but she lay down on the playroom sofa and fell asleep. Erwin and I marvelled again at her capacity to lose herself in the immediate moment, to sleep when tired, even on an occasion so intensely anticipated.

The studio was less impressive in reality than on the box. The children were packed in tiers on a skeletal structure of planks and tubing, and we mums were pushed into a corner, whence we had an obstructed sideways view. Sarah and Daniel, being among the youngest, were put in the front row – less danger of falling off in mid-performance. They sat absolutely still, and it's as well they weren't picked to answer any of the simple questions which were the specialty of the programme (What animal begins with D?), because even Sarah looked too hypnotised to answer.

When the show ended, the children lined up for a hand-out: a bottle of Coca-Cola, packets of salty junk titbits, a slice of fruit cake, an orange, a ruler, and a tin money-box from the State Savings Bank. The Happy Show team kept them in order with rough hands and steely voices, abruptly switching off the smiles worn for the cameras. Daniel ate most of his goodies in the car on the way home, and was sick on the kitchen floor. Sarah, who had made herself sick from over-eating once or twice before, drained her bottle of Coca-Cola, but saved up the packets of samples, without any hint from us, and opened them one at a time during the next few days.

For me, these and other special occasions were set apart by some unique intensity of happiness or discovery. There is no way of telling whether they were special for Sarah also. 'Everything was an occasion for her,' Erwin once remarked. 'I remember her jumping up and down with excitement because she was going to ride as far as the front gate with Grandpa in the Daimler.'

'One should be able to live always with that intensity', Cecily had said.

XVII

Reading lessons

After Sarah had returned to the Robert Cochrane, and I had accepted its bland atmosphere, I began teaching her to read myself. I hadn't at first thought of trying, since I had picked up the notion that it was a recondite and delicate task, best left to teachers. Then one day, in Cheshire's bookshop, I saw a book called *Why Johnny Can't Read,* described as an American best-seller. It turned out to be a scathing attack on the origins, theory, methods, and reading-books of the then-dominant 'Look and Say' approach, and a rumbustious proclamation of the eagerness of children to learn, and the ability of parents to teach. 'Teaching a child to read,' said the author, Rudolph Flesch, 'is very simple. Reading means getting meaning from certain combinations of letters. Teach the child what each letter stands for, and he can read.' This optimistic simplification got me started. A new ritual, the reading lesson, was added to our day.

It took place after lunch, and we began by lighting the sitting-room fire, after first going to the wood-pile at the back of the garden to fetch logs and mallee-roots. Sarah liked to pick out an exceptionally large and knobby mallee-root to carry. Then, eager but apprehensive, she demanded to be allowed to light the fire, and I struck a match for her and watched closely while she put it to the paper. As the flames flared and crackled, we sat side-by-side on the red chintz sofa and began the lesson.

I fumbled and groped my way towards a method. We started by using the alphabets and word lists at the back of Flesch's book, for the use of those who could not get hold of an old-fashioned reader. The alphabet was spaciously set out, in print and script, upper and lower case, and illustrated by words and drawings: Apple, arrow, bed, ball. I named each letter, demonstrated 'the sound it makes', and read out the two words it is 'for'. She repeated it all after me, and after one or two sessions could recite the lot without a mistake.

I thought she might be taking her cue from the pictures, rather than from the letters, so next I asked her to 'read' the alphabet from the end papers of the book, where there were no pictures. She had already accepted our first exploration of what a reading lesson was, and asked on succeeding days, 'Can we have apple and arrow?' But she raced through the unillustrated alphabet as fast as possible, reciting without looking. That didn't seem right either; I wanted her to *read*, looking at each letter as she named it, having a notion that part of my teacherly task was to help establish an indelible association between the shape of each letter and its sound.

To make her slow down and look at the shapes, I asked her to wait until I pointed to a letter, before she named it. The pointer was a pencil, knitting needle, straightened paper-clip, sliver of firewood, or implement from her set of modelling tools, whatever I could find. Sarah wanted a pointer too, so the ceremonial of the lesson now began with her choosing the best one. Then, wielding our pointers, we proceeded through the alphabet. As a reward for patience, I let her race through the last group, v w x y z. We continued to start each session with the alphabet, but moved on to words as well. The book set out whole pages of them in long close-printed columns, starting with lists of three-letter words, all containing the same vowel. Confidently, using my pointer, I asked her to read mat, ham, fan. . . She looked at me uncomprehendingly. I demonstrated how to sound out the letters and then 'run them together', in the time-honoured way, but when I asked her to try for herself, she hesitated, made mistakes, looked bored. Clearly that was no good.

Perhaps the difficulty was that each word contained three letters. If she had to identify only one letter at a time, it might be easier. I invented another drill. Moving to a page where all the vowels were used, I pointed to a word and gave her two alternatives. 'That is either big or bog. Which is it?' She enjoyed this new game and answered quickly, but wrong as often as right, clearly guessing.

I began to feel discouraged. If she didn't understand what reading was, I didn't understand what it was that she didn't understand. Flesch's lists looked forbiddingly long, and his procedure endless. 'Do each exercise until Johnny can read and write each word without the slightest hesitation.' (For the moment I ignored 'write'.) 'When you have done all the words horizontally from left to right, do them vertically. Do them from right to left. Do them from the bottom up, diagonally, and picking out words here and them at random. Make as sure as you can that Johnny can really read all the words. Do the exercises in the exact order in which they are printed. Otherwise you'll defeat your purpose.' So disaster (and boredom) threatened even in something 'very simple'.

Sarah wasn't discouraged though. She liked my guessing-game, and continued to ask, 'Can we have big and bog?' Later in the afternoon, I would hear her playing teacher to Daniel. Holding a book, any book, and a pointer, she would say with teacherly solemnity, 'Now Daniel, that is either pig or peg. Which is it?" Daniel dutifully replied one or the other and she rewarded him with a mimicked 'Good!'

Guessing wouldn't get us anywhere, but if I held her back at every word until she got it right, her eagerness would melt away. I could scent discouragement long before she did. If we had a shorter and less forbidding book, it might be easier to get her to look closely at the words, without making the game seem interminable. So next time I was in town, I went to an educational bookshop to look for a reading primer. Various series of books were displayed, all well printed, brightly coloured, cleverly illustrated. And all designed for the Look and Say heresy, starting off with stories of a sort, and giving a vocabulary count for each volume, so many words previously learned plus so many new ones. But I agreed with Flesch that she shouldn't be learning words, she should be learning to read.

Then, hidden away on a lower shelf, I found a series based on phonics, introducing words via letters and sounds.

I bought all six books of *Sounds and Words*, each with a prettily-striped cover, yellow and lilac, pink and green, blue and orange. They gave word lists too, but on smaller pages than Flesch's, in larger print, with fewer words to the page, and more space around each word. A drawing at the top of each page gave us a title for the lesson.

Page one started traditionally with Cat, and contained fifteen words – mat, fat, fan, Dan, once more. And once more I pointed to each in turn and asked her to read it. She still looked bewildered, guessed, hesitated, sounded the separate letters slowly and laboriously, but couldn't 'run them together', repeated a word after me when I demonstrated, but did no better with the next one. I felt torn between wanting her to look at each word until she saw what it meant, and the desire to protect her from failure and discouragement. The pragmatically reached solution was to keep moving forward. I began to accept any correct reading however reached, whether by her or me. Somehow, by the time we got to the end of *Page One, Cat,* she had succeeded in identifying two or three words by herself, probably more to my relief than to hers.

Mindful of Flesch's counsel of thoroughness, I asked her to read the page a second time, but she didn't want to, and when I insisted, stumbled as much as the first time. But sustaining her enthusiasm and hope seemed to me the first and absolute essential, so I stopped insisting on repetition. Indeed I saw that revision and mastering each lesson thoroughly before proceeding to the next, were dreary notions, which I have never myself followed when learning anything. And unnecessary, since the same sounds and letters will recur. So we went on, through Bed and Pig and Dog. She began to find it easier, sounded the letters without hesitation, and moved more quickly from disconnected sounds to words. Our lessons were short. I wanted to keep the atmosphere cheerful and companionable, and if I felt myself becoming impatient, or if she started to wriggle and squirm and talk of other things, I stopped for the day. On most days, she asked, 'Can I have a reading lesson?'

As well as lists of words, I tried to get her to read a story, for variety and because I imagined that her effort should be rewarded as early as possible by a continuous flow of meaning. I chose a book from her collection, a vacuous story of two bears dressed in shirts and trousers, the sort of cooked-up tale which I disliked, but which I selected because we hadn't previously read it. Reading Bears in Trousers was another flop. There were combinations of letters, *th* for example, which she hadn't yet learned. That didn't deter her, and she was very happy to read a story. At first she simply invented; later she must have asked Mama or Beverly to read it to her, and her retentive memory allowed her to reproduce it fairly accurately. She loved giving a bravura performance, like mine at bedtime. I, solemn pedant, didn't allow her to continue acting. But I could also see that it was no use insisting yet that she give an accurate reading, so Bears in Trousers was discarded.

For a while we confined ourselves to *Sounds and Words*, continuing on through the long vowels and simple combinations of consonants, through *oo* and *sh* and *ing*. She began to decipher the words quite quickly. No problem about *oo* having two pronunciations. I told her to try one way, and if that didn't make a word, to try the other, and she took to that easily. We finished Book One with a sense of achievement. After we had started on Book Two, I turned back a few times to Cat or Bed or Pig. She looked at the words silently, and then read the entire page without a mistake. But we didn't often go back because the pace had become quite fast, and she always liked to start a new page. The words became longer, and she read them with only slight hesitation between the syllables: trench-es, trav-ell-ing, um-brell-a, curr-ant bun. She would survey her progress, looking back at the pages conquered, and forward to those still to come. I hadn't taught her the numerals, but she knew them. 'Tomorrow we are going to do Page 12, Candle,' she said happily.

I didn't overhear her replaying with Daniel this stage in her progress. It couldn't be faked. She had made the transition from imagining herself a new being, a reader, to experiencing a new doing, reading, from an image of self to an encounter with the world. Sometimes, thinking of myself rather than of her, I see this transition as the essence of growing up, a discovery that is made once for all time. But that is an illusion; most of us have to go on learning it over and over again, to the end of life.

We started a new story, Horse, Book Two in one of those calculated schemes I had despised. Someone had given it to her for her birthday, and I had regarded it with scorn, but Daniel asked me to read it to him, and it occurred to me that I could use it in her lesson. Because of its simplicity, it was right for the stage she had reached.

Challenged to decipher Horse, her new insight into the nature of reading vanished again. She had learned that she must look closely at the letters on the page to find the images hidden in those single words; rabbit, button, carrot – images more vivid and surprising, more worth trying to decipher, than any in those uninspired stories for beginning readers. With *Horse*, she could be careless without missing anything, could read 'the' for 'this', 'were' for 'are', and, I suppose, 'Dora' for 'Dick'. I always stopped her and asked her to look again.

Before she finished the dreary marvellous text, I bought her another in the same series, Monkey, the next one that was available. I had given her many books, but this was the first for her to read herself. She caressed it, examined the pictures proudly, read out the title, and noted the serial number. 'Horse is Book Two and Monkey is Book Four. Why didn't you buy Book Three?' she asked.

One Saturday morning, as we were driving down Glenferrie Road towards the supermarket carpark, she pointed to a signboard. 'It says Health Food Shop,' she said.

I didn't try to teach her to write, although I knew that many theorists, including Maria Montessori, insisted that it should be learned at the same time as reading, or even earlier. But I have always found the physical act of writing laborious. I remembered how, in kindergarten, I had felt overburdened and hopeless as I struggled to copy a three-line caption from a picture in my reader. Nowadays I type even shopping lists, so I didn't expect her to enthuse about learning to write.

Months later, I found an exercise book I had once given her, one of those old-fashioned ones with liquorice-black covers, red edges, and thick creamy paper lined in pale blue. She had filled half of its pages with pencilled scribbles. Then came three words printed in wobbly capitals: M U M M Y, D A D D Y, S H E L L. It is her only written message, three words that summarise her world, for S H E LL might represent the four of us together, on outings to the country. I picture us on a quiet Sunday morning, filling up at a suburban garage, while Sarah hops out and dances round the station-wagon, before we head for Lilydale and the mountains.

XVIII

Bedtimes

Before she went home at half past five, the nurse bathed the children and put on their pyjamas and dressing gowns. Then while I got the dinner, they played together, or watched television with Grandpa. During the week, dinner-time was the one part of the day when we were all together, crammed into the kitchen, with Daniel's splay-legged highchair taking up most of the space between table and cooker. Müttchen ate with us and occasionally Grandpa, though usually I took him his meal on a tray.

Sarah, after years of eating extraordinarily little, suddenly developed a good appetite, and began to eat everything that was served. Impossible not to see refusal of food as refusal of love and of life itself. As I watched her polish off a big helping of carrots, I felt a great sense of relief, as if she had at last become an ordinary tough human being. She had never resembled the exemplary Spock child who, because she is never urged to eat her vegetables, just naturally likes them. She retained marked preferences though. When we had fish, she would eat a particularly large meal; and if I didn't watch her when she served herself to gravy, she would take more than her share. (I jotted down these facts years ago, but only now notice that fish and gravy are also particular likings of Erwin's.)

She understood the distinctions we made between different foods and different kinds of tableware, and always wanted the most ceremonious. So for a long time she insisted that her milk be served in one of the cut-crystal glasses inherited from my mother, which we used for guests. After three had been broken, for she was apt to knock things off the table with awkward movements, we refused to let her have them. Then she used a glass with a kookaburra on it that Beverly had given her, or one from a set decorated with fruit that Grandpa had won as a golf trophy, the one with grapes, whose gold rim was still shiny. Our white porcelain tea cups chipped easily, so we bought similarly-shaped earthenware ones for the children, but Sarah wouldn't use them. She noticed whenever her drink was give in one, and demanded, 'I want a cup like yours.'

Dinner times could be a trial. Sarah talked, or sang incessantly in a loud voice, and climbed on Erwin, or demanded that he feed her. Daniel was cheerfully rowdy, and they egged each other on to defy our attempts at imposing order. Rather feeble attempts, because we were conscious that during the day they had been segregated for the sake of our other interests, so it seemed right that they should get some of their own way at night. We never succeeded in being stern for long enough to be taken seriously.

What began as a celebration of our being together could expand into an orgy of showing-off, defiant wildness, or persecution. 'Let's torture old Dad, he doesn't mind!'

and they both climbed on him, ruffled his hair and poked their fingers into his ears and eyes. Or Sarah went to collect Grandpa's tray and raced spectacularly back with it, the dishes bouncing and sliding. Or she chose this moment to go to the lavatory, and called out to me, 'I've done a poo and a wee, and I need cleaning up!' They didn't continuously behave like this, only at dinner-time, and then never if guests were present. And at the end of a long day in the country, when they were tired, and I drove so that Erwin could bear the brunt of their tumbling and pummelling.

We had our own private reprimands: "Noggs, you're a boggs!' or 'Don't be boggsish!' No doubt it was more for our own sakes than for theirs that we avoided the overtones of 'naughty', though it did serve to distinguish our condemnations from those of other people. The reproof was delivered lightly, half jokingly, but it was recognised as such. 'I'm not a boggs!' one of them sometimes objected.

We rarely went out at night, because she hated it. When we did, we told her days beforehand, so that there would be no sudden surprise. Sometimes then her eyes filled with tears and she said, 'I don't want you to go. Don't go!' At other times she asked quite calmly, 'Who is going to look after me?' Margot, Robin and Beverly were all prepared to baby-sit, so we never had to call in an unknown sitter. And she always had Daniel as her ally and companion in the child-world, from within whose solidarity they confronted any alien night-time presence.

When the moment came for us to leave, she would sometimes wave goodbye with stoical self-control and a demand that we come home early; at others, she clung to us and cried bitterly. We both felt rent by her distress. Erwin said it spoiled all his pleasure in going out. One night, when friends called for us in their car, and she stood weeping in the doorway as we drove off, the other wife commented, 'Children are awful little moral blackmailers, aren't they?' Her cold detachment shocked me; I could never have made such a remark. But I knew that after we had gone, as the baby-sitters reported, Sarah would immediately regain her cheerfulness and interest in whatever was happening.

On ordinary days at home, the children's dinner-time boisterousness evolved into the marvellous after-dinner game of Chasey. We had only to appear in one of the four doorways that linked the downstairs rooms, and call out 'Chasey', to start them off. 'Look out, Daniel,' Sarah called. 'They're coming! Run for your life!' She was the more agile, darting and changing direction like a hare, while Daniel trotted stolidly after her. When we pulled the obvious trick of appearing suddenly in front of them instead of behind, Sarah turned so swiftly that she cannoned into Daniel, and they collapsed softly like a pair of puppies. We hardly needed to do more than step from one foot to the other, for them to race off again, encouraging each other with screams that were both gleeful and apprehensive. Sarah loved Erwin to catch her, and she would run full tilt into his arms, go limp so that he couldn't hold her, then wriggle free and be off again. Or, instead, she would call, 'He's an old camel. Get up beast! Gee-up! Hey-up!' in a broad rustic accent copied from Erwin. The beast, swaying and rocking under his double load, and belaboured with fists and heels, pounded round the room on all fours, while I had a welcome rest, and we all laughed.

Going upstairs was a game too. Erwin had to 'frog them', or they would 'walk like little spiders'. At the top, the mood changed, more or less. Sarah cleaned her teeth solemnly, like a good little girl, but Daniel, developing an independent role as a buffoon, sometimes painted the walls with his wet tooth brush, or clowned around until, immense success, he landed with both feet in the toilet bowl. Then, after the exuberance, came a slow winding-down. Two stories from each of us, sitting on Sarah's bed, one for her, and another, simpler and preferably about trains or boats, often chosen by Sarah, for Daniel. I tucked them both in and said goodnight, left the room while Erwin in turn read stories and said goodnight, and returned again for a last reassurance. The final farewell was the most ritualised part of bedtime, a sequence of formulae and gestures which must be repeated every night, although it did slowly change, new phrases being added and others eventually dropped.

Sarah: 'Is the light like I always have it?' (It always was, and she didn't look, or listen to the answer.) 'Goodnight, Sarahkin darling,' I kissed her, but if I didn't kiss her full on the mouth, she would pull my head around, or say, 'I want to kiss your mouth.' This was part of Erwin's goodnight too, and we thought she had learned it from television. We were both uncertain how we should respond, and independently decided to kiss her on the mouth, but lightly and casually. She often raced through the final words, but never omitted them. 'Make sure I'm nicely tucked up before you clean your teeth, and after. See you later, alligator.' For a time the ritual ended there, until she added a final sentence which had originally belonged only to Erwin's goodnight: 'See you in the morning when we have breakfast together.'

After the light had finally been turned out, I remained lying on my bed in the next room for a few minutes, to make sure that all was quiet before I went downstairs. I felt very close to them then.

(Notebook, 25.1.69) Add to my account of bedtime rituals, thoughts from tonight when I was putting Daniel to bed. His ritual goes on too long, or rather he postpones it for too long, so that by the time we reach it I am impatient, and listen with edgy detachment. One listens most of the time with love and sympathy, because of one's closeness and knowledge of the importance to them. But sometimes, if the love is less near the surface, or the demands are greater, only after a conscious effort to master impatience, and with faked interest. But Sarah never pushed me to that extreme. If she saw me becoming impatient, she would rush through the ritual cheerfully. Out of sensitivity to my mood, but also from self-protection. Completing it was important to her.

Occasionally I did become impatient, but on most nights I felt so identified with her that I was equally absorbed in the ceremony. She would gabble through it for other reasons too – if I said I was tired, or if we had guests downstairs, or if we were going out after dinner. Then extra questions were added:

Are you just going to have a cup of coffee and then come home?

Yes, that's all.

If there are any sweets, will you bring me some?

Yes, I will.

Will you come and see me as soon as you get home and read me a story if I'm awake.

Yes, of course. (But she never was.)

I describe her demands and inventions not Daniel's. It was certainly she who dictated the order of ceremony; her anxieties seemed stronger than his. Because he hadn't yet reached the age when end-of-day conflicts are strongest, or because he had never had to face them without her companionable presence?

It seems odd that children should be boisterous at the end of the day. Perhaps it is the body's instinctive way of ensuring sleep by using up the remainder of the day's energy. But those furious displays of energy often seemed the product of tiredness itself. It was when they were already exhausted, after an eventful day, or on the way home from a long outing, that they became almost hysterically wild, as if drawing on reserves of nervous energy not ordinarily needed. The strenuous refusal to acknowledge that the day is over increases tiredness, but tiredness unlocks the energy for a still wilder rejection. Usually, the spiral ends with the change to ritual, but occasionally it goes out of control. There were nights when I could not calm them, when they were seized by a mounting excitement that only tears could release.

I thought that Erwin did not understand this; he could recklessly urge them on to greater wildness. He once said that he did not believe there was such a state as overtiredness. Such blindness was possible because he didn't have the ultimate responsibility for getting them to bed. He said his goodnights and left. It was my job to wait until they were asleep.

Complicity in a bedtime ritual can seem to a parent like one side of a bargain in which the child's whims are indulged, in return for her acceptance that in due course she will be abandoned to the night. But the conflict is not just between parent and child. The conflict was within her too. It was hard for her to tear herself way from the day's involvements, but she needed and wanted sleep. The nightly ritual prepares for sleep through its ordered familiarity. Boisterous play is unpredictable and shapeless, and has no natural climax. Ritual is structured and self-contained and moves to a foreseeable end. It has the completeness of a work of art.

Two other bedtime conversations remain in my memory. The first took place one night close to Sarah's fifth birthday. 'I don't want to die,' Sarah said. 'You won't die for a long long time darling,' I replied. 'You'll grow up and go to school and have lots of fun and learn all sorts of things, and then you'll go to the University. . .' She interrupted me. 'I don't want to go to the University. I only want to be a mother.'

I don't think she meant simply a mother like me, but the mother she felt within herself. She already understood maternal yearning, and could imagine herself absorbed in tender care for a tiny vulnerable being. Friends who saw her with younger children often commented that she was already a little mother.

On the night of this conversation, I felt pleased that I had avoided the lie direct, 'You won't have to die!' which mothers equally devoted to the truth have sometimes felt compelled to give. And I might have remembered this exchange with gentle amusement at the decisive way in which she rejected my vision of her future, and announced her own. After her death, I brooded over my reply, and changed my judgment of myself several times. In appalled astonishment, I recognised that my answer had also been a lie, or at least an evasion. How, I asked myself, could I have assured Sarah so blandly that her death lay far off in the scarcely imaginable future. I felt that I had betrayed both her and the truth. Then I gave myself the excuse that I had merely omitted a 'probably', which it would be pedantic to insist on. Finally after meditating many times on this exchange, I came to recognise with humility that, like those mothers who said, 'You need not die. You can live for ever,' my longing to reassure her had been stronger than my concern for truth. And rightly so.

Another conversation was repeated many times, an occasional part of our bedtime ritual. Sarah would ask apprehensively, 'Are there any wolves and foxes?' and I would reassure her, 'No, there are no wolves and foxes.' I came to condemn this, too, as a lie, although a less obvious one, the lie poetic, a lie in metaphoric disguise and so open to varying interpretations. The one uppermost in my mind at the time was, that no death-dealing power would come to attack her in the night, that very night whose darkness already surrounded us. I am fairly certain that this is what she too meant. So my reply is open to the same accusation and the same defence as the previous one.

But the metaphor has a second meaning for me, and a different reassurance is hidden in my reply. 'There are no wolves and foxes' rejected the view that the world is essentially a place of cruelty and injustice. And is that a lie? Sometimes I think so, sometimes not; but if it is, then it is a lie I would still tell her. Not 'You need never die!' Not, as Arthur Koestler thought children needed to believe, 'There is a God.' But 'Love and courage are stronger than evil and chaos.'

XIX

Portrait of a Five-Year-Old

When I started to write about Sarah, I resolved to show her through an accumulation of incident and detail drawn from memories that were still vivid, rather than through broad generalisation. I soon discovered that I remembered much less than I had hoped and believed. Especially for her first years, most of the precise actuality of living with her was already lost beyond recall. Often, what had at first seemed to be a memory of her turned out to be a recollection of my own emotions, or the hazy evocation of an atmosphere. So what I have written up to this point is a slice of autobiography and a narrative of family life as much as a biography of Sarah. For the last year of her life, however, my memories of her are more copious and detailed. Arranged under a number of headings, they add up to a portrait of Sarah at the age of five.

Birthday
For Sarah's fifth birthday, I gave a party to which we invited the children of friends, and fellow pupils from the Robert Cochrane whose names Sarah had given me. I hired a pony for their entertainment. 'I'm going to have a pony at my party,' Sarah announced loudly on arriving at

school. I reminded her that not all the children would be coming to the party, and it wasn't polite to boast in front of the others about what they would be missing. 'It's hard for them to understand,' the teacher said. But I didn't think it was hard, if one thought to explain. She didn't again talk about the party in front of children not invited.

She came with me to order the birthday cake from a shop Betty recommended, whose cakes were decorated with elaborate scenes drawn in icing. Sarah hesitated for a long time over her choice, before plumping for The Three Bears again, the same as last year, 'And next year I'll have Red Riding Hood.'

On the day of the party, the man with the pony turned up early, and Sarah rode around the garden talking to him, until the guests arrived. It was a reasonably successful party, though it taught me how to give a better one. A basic lesson is that the party tea must be served early; food acts like alcohol on small children; after it they are gayer and more relaxed. And one must be alert to cues as to how rituals should be performed, lest the initiation be invalid. Sarah burst into tears because I struck up Happy Birthday before the candles were blown out instead of after, and we had to sing it a second time.

I've always been sceptical about presents. It seems almost impossible in our wantonly productive society to give anything that fulfils a real desire. I see those children, fresh and pretty in their best clothes, each holding a gaily wrapped parcel, as another example of the doomed optimism which so wrenches one's heart living with children. But Sarah received a number of presents that gave her pleasure, books which I would not have thought of buying, and items of clothing I considered superfluous.

After her birthday, there was a new ceremoniousness to her departure for school. Wearing a plaid dress with a white collar, which she named her School Dress, three strings of enormous pink pearls chosen by a friend, whose desire to please was not inhibited by my scruples about good taste, and her new red and white Norwegian gloves, and carrying her umbrella, another present, she walked to the Boddington car with an air of conscious dignity.

For our present, she asked for a Bride Doll. I hadn't known such a thing existed, but the Glenferrie Road toy shop had a range of them, from which we chose a pretty dark-haired bride bedecked with lace and orange blossom. Sarah seldom took any of her possessions to school, although other children often did. When I asked her why she never took one of the bears, she replied, 'He might get lost.' But she took the Bride Doll, which belonged to the new order of values learned outside the family. It sat enthroned on top of the piano, in all the glory of its spreading, paper-white dress and veil.

The acstress, we called her, using Sarah's word. Playing the hostess, as she ran to open the door to friends, or handed round the nuts or the cakes, or said as they left, 'I'm so glad you could come.' None of it was prompted. She modelled herself on us, of course, but we thought that she didn't simply give a slavish imitation, but caught the sense of the occasion. It needs, in so young a child, or in anyone, abundant confidence and a strong sense of self to play a part without feeling obliterated by it, without creating a split between the acting self and the real self. It doesn't have to become a matter of 'people who confront each other in masks'; Sarah the acstress remained exuberantly herself.

She taught Müttchen to 'be an ugly old witch'. At first Müttchen said she couldn't possibly, as if she were asked to be really wicked. But with teasing from us and urging from Sarah she learned, in her seventies, with fading memory and limited English, to become convincing new beings: the ugly old witch, the patient during their hour-long games of Dr Poss, the modern mother.

I didn't play many such roles, but I had one speciality, improvised for a practical reason. Erwin or I cut her hair but she never wanted to sit still long enough for us to do it properly, hence the ragged look it has in many photographs. But I discovered a way of getting her cooperation by playing a farcical hairdresser, with a simpering voice and affected gestures, flourishing the scissors and standing back to admire her. 'What beautiful hair you have, Miss Fabian. I may truly say it is a pleasure to cut such hair. Now if you would just be so kind as to turn your head this way for a moment while I adjust a few ends, I promise that you will look utterly ravishing. 'Thank you, Miss Fabian.' It was a successful performance. 'Be a hairdresser,' she would command me.

Sarah loved to transform herself into a parody of furious anger. She clenched her fists, bared her lower teeth and shook her head violently. I don't know who originated this piece of mime, but both Erwin and I copied it if we wanted to show disapproval of something one of the children had done – or, more likely, left undone, or done badly, or too slowly. Sarah enjoyed our act, but our transformation into distorted monsters was also frightening, and after a moment she would say, 'Be a friendly mummy!' Sometimes I countered with a saccharine smile, and then she would ask for another inoculation of anger, 'Be cross again!' The second time, my performance would be greeted with laughter.

She copied another gesture of mine. Faced with some minor disaster – no milk, a forecast of rain, a favourite shirt dyed mauve in the wash – I would express my rueful acknowledgment by nodding my head rapidly. Sarah turned this mannerism into a piece of grotesque clowning entirely her own. She pushed out her lower lip, opened her eyes in a wide stare, and moved her head from side to side, nodding emphatically. It looked savage and rather mad. And she used this performance not just to comment on a disappointment, but as an abstract statement, which she might make at any time and before any company. Often at mealtimes, sitting at the table, apropos of nothing. I see it as a declaration, both tragic and cheerful, of her acceptance of an imperfect universe.

Tears

Sarah wasn't a cry-baby. Her tears never lasted long, and she did not use them to manipulate or punish us. Nevertheless, at five she would still break into tears, briefly but tempestuously, at sudden changes of fortune or unexpected disappointments: when we were leaving to go out to dinner, or if denied some anticipated treat. For a while, she used to ask for and be given an ice cream when we went to the corner shops, until we decided that it was happening too often for her good, and that there would be no more ice creams. On the next three or four occasions, there were tears at our refusal, and then the new pattern was accepted.

Small babies have few ways of expressing their reactions: smiles and gurgles, or desperate wails, but little in between. I think that as children grow and acquire an increasingly subtle knowledge of words, they learn varying ways to express pleasure, before they achieve a similar control over disappointment. Sarah lived with such an intensity of joy and anticipation that a sudden thwarting overwhelmed her, and she could master it only through tears. Once, when an evening parting had been particularly tearful, I asked her next day, 'You didn't really mind us going, did you? You knew we would come back.' 'Yes, but I liked to cry,' Sarah replied.

Clothes and pretty things
A parcel arrived from Ruth containing a dress for her birthday. She put it on at once, and admired herself in the bedroom mirror, but not for long. Her attention never remained turned-in on herself, but quickly reached out to others. She ran to share her pleasure with Grandpa, and danced in front of him, in the white dress sprigged with tiny red flowers and the black tights I had recently given her. They were her first and she was very proud of them.

Daniel, at the same age, greeted my return from town by

asking 'Have you brought me a present?' 'Not today!' I replied. But then, a few minutes later, 'I've just remembered, I did bring you something. I brought you a new pair of trousers.' Daniel, furious, burst into tears. 'I didn't want those trousers!'

Sarah usually had a dress for special occasions, her Party Dress. Often on ordinary days she would ask, 'Can I wear my Party Dress?' but I only agreed if it was nearly ready to be washed. Her first party dress was turquoise velveteen, and I made it for Christmas, just before we left London, recalling the blue velvet dresses with lace collars that Betty and I had worn as children. The dress I made looked clumsy, too wide for its length, and it wasn't finished in time for Christmas, but two years later it fitted her better. Beverly lengthened it with a wide band that almost matched, covering the join with white fringe; it looked old-world and pretty. Sarah often asked to wear it, until she got her new winter party dress of brilliant pink velveteen. After that, she never asked to wear the old one.

Most of the time she wore corduroy overalls, which were given names: Work Pants, Leopard Pants, Grass Pants. Then, when she was nearly five, she began wanting to wear dresses all the time. She and Daniel had just begun explicitly to identify figures in their story books as girls, if they were wearing dresses. She wore a dress to school, but when we went to the country, I insisted on pants, because she got so dirty. She would readily agree if she knew that I was wearing them too (this being before trousers became ubiquitous wear for women.)

She noticed the distinctions we made among our own clothes. 'Why have you got your town clothes on?' she asked when I began to wear last year's jersey suit at home. When she saw Erwin in his best pullover, she patted it and said, 'You are naughty, to wear your good pullover for work.' 'Are you going to wear a sleeveless dress?', she asked me. If I were, she insisted that she should too.

She began to be aware of fashion, pushing her cardigan sleeves up to the elbow in the casually chic way, and asking me to buy the latest accessory, a knitted hair band. I bought her a red one, which she wore every day for weeks. A little later she asked for gloves, but something in me didn't approve; clothes should be pretty, but also practical and necessary, and it wasn't cold enough to need gloves. To her delight, someone gave her a pair for her birthday.

She hoarded a collection of scraps of material, short remnants which my mother had at some time brought home from the factory, odd-shaped pieces left over from cutting out her clothes, bits of towelling from the ragbag, and a beautiful piece of cerise silk, which she sometimes tied around her waist. 'My covers' she called this collection, and a bundle of them had to come with us whenever we travelled. The stray black cat, which we had adopted at her insistence, slept on her doll's bed, on a 'blanket' made from one of these covers, which she had folded carefully and precisely to fit the bed.

She liked a pretty cover on her own bed too, and resisted any change. When, on cold nights, I put an extra blanket on top of her flowered quilt, she objected strongly. She always lay very neatly in bed, with the Piggy Pillow that Klaus and Julie had sent her on one side, and Bear, the newest and most handsome of the bears, on the other.

(Notebook 24.6.64) On the table beside her bed when I dusted it this morning was a neat little pile: three copies of a leaflet about the koala bear which she had collected on a visit to the Healesville Sanctuary and which she call a 'map'; another leaflet about the platypus; a subscription-offer card from Time magazine with a drawing of a bird, which she had been anxious I shouldn't tear; a postcard of a koala like those we had sent to friends at Christmas, and another of a dog with a baby koala on its back sent to her by American friends; some copper coins and a French five-franc piece; a handkerchief printed with lilies of the valley, and a box of paper tissues, which she knew were not as good as hankies; if offered one she would say, 'No, I want a real hanky.' These things were arranged tidily on the bottom shelf. On the top was a grotesque inflated plastic doll, given her by my mother. She kept nothing else on the top shelf except the book she had been reading before she went to sleep; she always asked me to put other books on the dressing table before I switched out the light.

'Ladies'

We had fed the swans in the Botanical Gardens. 'Do you want to go to the Ladies?' I asked her. She nodded, so we left Erwin and Daniel to wait under a spreading Moreton Bay fig tree, and walked up the hill to a low brick building half-concealed by a rockery planted with yuccas. Sarah went inside matter-of-factly and performed as required, but when she came out, she asked, surprised, balanced between expectation and disappointment, 'But where are the Ladies?' Shadowy terrors lurk, we know, beneath every child's familiar daylit world, but so do radiant expectations. How marvellous to be so filled with hope that a single word can conjure up, behind the Botanical Gardens tea kiosk, a drawing-room where silken countesses are taking tea!

Soon after this, she developed a passion for visiting public lavatories, which are generously provided in Australian towns. For a while, they were the focal point for her exploration of the world, and the test of her courage to venture into it alone. It began one brilliant morning in early summer, after I had taken the children to the dentist. The occasion was ceremonious. Sarah and I wore our prettiest cotton dresses, and Daniel a white Italian suit someone had sent him. Leighton West, whom I had known since I was a schoolgirl, wanted to make their introduction to his profession an auspicious one. With jovial courtesy, he demonstrated the chair's tricks, and showed them his probes and mirrors, a colleague from down the corridor was summoned to meet them, we were given coffee in the back room, and a nurse escorted us to the lift and waited with the children while I fetched the car.

To mark the occasion further, and because it was a splendid day, we went to the beach. We put on our swimsuits in a deserted changing shed, whose bleached benches and sandy floor were as clean as ocean-scoured driftwood. When we emerged, Sarah announced that she wanted a wee. Waving her hand towards one of the brick blocks set at intervals in the middle of the road, between the Victorian villas with glassed-in verandahs and the pale sea, 'I can go by myself,' she said. I watched her dance along the footpath and cautiously cross the road, and waited until she came out and ran back towards me, her face bright with achievement.

Before that, she used to strip off her swimming trunks defiantly, spread her feet wide, and pee on the sand in full view of everyone. And I recall an earlier occasion, on our first trip to the mountains behind Melbourne. Late in the afternoon, as the light was beginning to fade, I sought out a farm which used to serve afternoon tea, decades before, when we stayed nearby during school holidays. It was till there, its ramshackle wooden buildings unchanged. We ordered tea with scones and jam and cream, and while we waited I walked round the garden with Sarah. Behind a hedge, in the damp pungent air, looking across a valley to the darkening bush, she weed among the cabbages, with an expression of such intense concentration and glee that it seemed like a libation of thanksgiving.

In late summer, when we made an overnight trip to Gippsland, she insisted on going alone, every time we stopped the car. At the motel she announced an urgent need already while we were booking in, and I said irritably that I didn't think there was one. 'Yes, there is,' she said, pointing to a door identified by the silhouette of a lady in a crinoline. Next morning, when we stopped for petrol at a small garage five minutes after setting out, she spotted a door marked 'Toilet', and got out to visit it.

Sarah set off to each of these places as if she expected to find the secret of life.

Daniel

Sarah and Daniel were physically very alike, with the same smooth tawny skin and rose-flushed cheeks, the same sturdy rounded bodies. I used to find it surprising that they resembled each other more than they did either of us – but then they had a common ancestry, whereas with each of us they shared only half an ancestry. But I wasn't in the habit of searching for likenesses and I didn't often perceive them. She was always, more than our child, a miracle sprung from nowhere. Only years later do I sometimes see her looking at me from Erwin's face, and even now I don't know what features of mine she had. But I noted very early that she had Erwin's hands, broad powerful hands with short tapering fingers. Hers were a delicate miniature version, especially touching because they were an exception to the classic infant beauty of her features.

Sarah and Daniel spent more time with each other than with either of us. I was only rarely away from them overnight, but they, from the time that Daniel was six weeks old, were never separated for a single night. Sarah went to school in the morning, and Daniel still had an afternoon nap, but the rest of the day was shared. Together they formed the child world, an enclave of love and safety more predictable and egalitarian than the wider realm of parent power. In the child world, they were allies against the universe. Its boundaries were constantly expanding, but it existed from the moment when Sarah took her new-born brother in her arms and looked down at him proudly and tenderly. He transformed her world.

As they grew, I think that Sarah's love and protectiveness

towards Daniel became stronger, and her jealousy, never corrosively sharp, faded. She retained the advantage of being older and superior in strength, knowledge and cunning, and she naturally took most of the leading roles, from Mum to Chief Conspirator. Overheard from the playroom: 'Now, Daniel, you stay there while I go to the office to make some money. I've got an appointment with Ossie Burt. Then I'll come home.'

Before Christmas, Sarah was taken out by Miss Lee, the buyer for the Ground Floor, whom she knew only from brief meetings while we waited for the lift. I had agreed to Miss Lee's invitation against my better judgment. Sarah had rarely gone out without us, but I was hypnotised, as scores of Flinders Lane wholesalers must have been, by Miss Lee's confident voice and lofty bearing, as she swept towards me like a trireme about to run down a coracle. The outing was a success. They braved the throngs in Bourke Street, walked through Myers, and had lunch in a coffee shop where, Miss Lee reported, Sarah behaved with mature self-possession. Although unfamiliar company and strange sights must nevertheless have strained her composure, she had insisted on finding the right present for her brother. She arrived home with a flushed triumphant face, clutching an inflated plastic elephant as big as herself, and asking, 'Where's Daniel?'

Sarah watched over Daniel's safety when they were out together. In the Glenferrie market, she held his hand to make sure he didn't wander away while Erwin was buying fruit and vegetables. I observed them once, when they were unaware of being watched, while we were picnicking at a remote spot in the mountains, and they wanted to cross the road to explore a timber-cutter's hut. Not a car had passed in the hour we had been there, but Sarah held Daniel back with her arm while she looked to right and left, before hurrying him across.

He followed her lead unquestioningly. When she slid on her stomach down the highest slide at Studley Park, he climbed up after her, although his legs could scarcely reach from one rung to the next.

At mealtimes, she was always impatient to leave the table after eating. 'May I go now and you call me when sweets are up?' And however heartily he was eating, Daniel would immediately down spoon and follow her.

Daniel stuck his finger into a chocolate cake in the delicatessen, and we had to buy it for him. 'Too young to know he shouldn't,' I thought. Sarah of course got one too; but later, the owner of the shop told us he had seen her nudge and encourage Daniel. But whose idea was it when they tipped the ash bucket over themselves, and rubbed cinders into their hair and clothes? I was cross with them that time. So was Erwin when they rolled a whole case of apples one at a time down the drive. And another time, when 'I'd left them in the car while I finished the shopping, with treats for all, marzipan and boxes of strawberries and loganberries. When I got back, all the sweets had been demolished, and Daniel had nibbled at fistfuls of berries from each of the boxes, and the car looked a terrible mess. Sarah had not been caught in the act of eating, and she said, "Look what your son has done!" I was furious with both of them.' These incidents stand out because of their rarity. They were seldom destructive, more often just cheerfully rebellious.

Daniel slept in a bed for the first time when we stayed in a motel at Lorne, in a family suite, with a back bedroom separated from the main room by a short passageway. We put the children to bed in the back room and settled down to read. A few minutes later we heard scuffling noises and then, 'Chuff-chuff, chuff-chuff, chuff-chuff, chuff-chuff,' they came marching in one behind the other, Daniel in front, cheeks puffed out and knees lifted high. Sarah must have learned at kindergarten to make such a stylish train. We laughed, and took them back to bed, but seconds later the performance was repeated again, and then again. Their solemnity changed to laughter, and our laughter to a severity that lacked conviction. 'That's the last time. Stay in bed now, and go to sleep!' But they re-appeared several more times before tempers flared, and then suddenly they were asleep.

They never had serious physical fights (perhaps those come later), but occasionally one of them dealt the other a quick sharp slap, or a bite on the arm which left tooth-marks. Sarah made no attempt at concealment. 'Why is Daniel crying?' I asked. 'I bit him,' she replied. But she had symbolic ways of asserting superiority, such as her version of a rhyme my mother used to sing:

Early in the morning, when we go up to London,
See the little puff-puff standing on the line.
The man in the engine pulls the little Daniel,
Toot-toot, puff-puff, off we go.

She liked to refer to him in a gently mocking, distancing

way: 'The boy's spilt his milk,' or, 'Your son's taken an apple.' Daniel sometimes came to Erwin's studio with an armful of sticks, or some tools; Erwin named him the engineer, and Sarah echoed, giggling, 'Here comes the engineer. He's going to make a complete check-up.' But when, at a children's party, she came to tell Erwin, 'I think Daniel's having difficulty with his ice cream,' she wasn't flaunting her superiority, but showing the same concern as the adults who hover round the edges of a children's party, anxious to make sure everyone is enjoying it.

'Once,' Erwin told me, 'Daniel broke a glass by throwing it on the floor, and I got absolutely furious, and hit him. Sarah remembered it, and quite some time afterwards she said to me, "You hit my brother. You shouldn't do that." But I knew immediately that it was wrong, and I felt terrible. It is totally useless and only shows how disgusting one is oneself, to do such a thing, to hit someone less than half your size because of a glass.'

For our bedtime story, the last ritual of the day, we all sat on Sarah's bed. Sometimes Daniel hurried to finish first in the bathroom, so that he could take possession of her bed, pulling the blankets up to his chin with a triumphant smile. Sarah would say, 'That's my bed, Daniel. Get out at once!' smugly, pleased to possess a right over him which she didn't intend to enforce. But sometimes she tried to push him out, and there would be a scuffle. Daniel would hit her quite hard, with fists or feet, a few times hard enough to make her cry, but at others, when I thought he was too rough, she first complained in a mock-adult tone, and then when I told him to stop, said, 'But I like it!' Occasionally these romps became cheerfully sexual. 'Tickle my tail, Daniel,' she would say encouragingly. 'Come on, stick your finger right in!'

Aunt Nell asked me to choose a book she could give Sarah at Christmas, and I bought one containing a story I myself had loved, *The Snow Queen*. Sarah was bored by it, but another story in the book did interest her, a Russian tale about two royal children, Ivan, who was mute, and his baby sister, an ogress with steel teeth. One day, Ivan came home to find his baby sister sitting in the ruins of the castle, whining:

I ate my father, I ate my mother,
I'm getting hungry to eat my brother.

Then the Infant Ogress clashed her teeth until sparks flew and the air rang with noise. She swelled up with rage until she was bigger than the castle. She stamped it into dust and started out after Ivan. He heard her as he galloped, and looked back. Her eyes shot lightning bolts, her teeth clanged, as she ran in her infant's bonnet and dress on enormous legs that went even faster than the black stallion's.

A truly horrific sister! But the story also contained charming episodes, and ended happily for Ivan. I hadn't censored other stories of violence and cruelty, accepting the theory that the terrors of folk tales do not outmatch children's own fantasies; so it didn't occur to me to censor this one, and Sarah asked for it every night for a week. Then something unprecedented happened; she started to wake up crying in the night. Perhaps those steel teeth were really too fearsome. I stopped reading *The Infant Ogress*, and once more Sarah slept soundly until morning.

A second brother-and-sister story, *Hansel and Gretel*, became a favourite with both of them. It might seem just as terrifying, with its murderous step-mother, cowardly father, and witch who forces Gretel to stoke the fire on which Hansel is to be cooked. But this time, brother and sister are allies, saved by their loving concern for each other. Sarah didn't wake in the night after hearing Hansel and Gretel. She and Daniel chanted its rhymes, laughing, with their heads close together:

Nibble, nibble like a mouse;
Who's that nibbling at my house?

(Notebook 1964) Our overnight stay in Lorne earlier this year. In the morning, I walked to the pier with the children, while Erwin and Müttchen did the shopping. That walk is imbued in my mind with something very characteristic of Sarah. Dignity? Yes, except that the word suggests something unchildlike, unduly grave and subdued, and Sarah certainly wasn't unchildlike. But she became totally absorbed in what she was doing, as if her whole being were concentrated in it, and in the joyful awareness of the occasion. That gave it an unforced ceremoniousness.

This walk to the pier was for Daniel. The fishing boats returned in the morning, and as each crew finished cleaning its catch and swilling down the boat, it came in close, and was lifted out of the water and stowed neatly on the pier by a small crane, operated by two fishermen; one hooked the crane onto the boat and watched to see that it didn't swing into the piles on its way up, while the other operated the winch. Daniel loved this. He had seen it before, on a previous visit to Lorne, and talked about it often, re-enacting the noises of the crane, and the way the boats swung around. Sarah was never interested in such mechanical matters, but she understood Daniel's enthusiasms, and liked to help him enjoy them.

So the focus of her attention as we walked along the narrow cliff path on that fresh sunny morning was Daniel, and her concern that he should be given this special treat. While we waited for the fleet to come in, we watched some men fishing from the end of the pier, and Sarah tried to talk to them, but received only gruff replies. Then we saw that a boat had arrived, and the three of us sat together at the side of the jetty while it was lifted out of the dark water.

Erwin

When I first resolved to write about Sarah, I tried to increase my hoard of true fragments of her life by asking friends to write down their memories of her. I had imagined that they could easily give me little documentary notes about particular occasions, like those I was myself making.

The attempt was a total failure; what was a necessity for me proved difficult and embarrassing for them. Most people didn't send me anything; a few wrote general impressions of her. Which I am glad to have, but they were not what I had hoped for.

I could not have questioned Erwin in this deliberate way, but sometimes I recorded comments from our conversations about her. So these words of his have a different status from anything I can now say in my own voice, writing to bear witness in public. They are private, spontaneous, and spoken when her living presence was still close, words that belong in life more completely than even the most unselfconscious of my notes.

'People used to think I was mad to spend so much time with her. Even years ago, when I went home every afternoon while you were ill, so that I could take her out instead of Nanny. But I don't regret any of it. I'd do exactly the same again.'

'I never broke a promise to her. She knew it. If I said I would bring her something, I did .'

'She always noticed anything that had been done for her. She would say, joyfully, "You've fixed it! Thank you, Daddy. Thank you very much." No-one ever told her to say that. I loved doing things for her. I bought a little pair of jeweller's pliers to mend her necklace. She hadn't even seen it yet.'

'Occasionally I lost my temper with her, and afterwards I'd be sorry. But lately she didn't take much notice when that happened. She was like a woman in love who accepts the bad moods of her lover indulgently.'

He told me about the stories he used to invent for her. They began with the possums at Portsea, during the winter when we were alone there. The nights were dark and cold and the house was isolated; we could hear no sounds of traffic or people, only the wind tossing the trees, and the waves on the beach below. Then suddenly possums would walk over the galvanised iron roof, with a noise like men in big boots. Sarah was terrified, and clung to Erwin in fear when he went to say goodnight. He explained that the possums were really rather nice small furry animals with big eyes, who were playing games on the roof. After that, they often looked for possums in trees and up telegraph poles, though they only once saw one, when Erwin shook a tree and the possum, which had been sleeping in the top branches, poked its head out.

His first story was about a cheeky possum who ate cherries, and threw the stones at the elephant while it slept. The elephant looked up and called out, 'Who is it?' and the possum said, 'Not me!' Sarah would call out rather tremulously, 'Not me!' Other stories were about a bear, a furry koala like the toys she carried tucked under her arm. 'Do the bear!' she would demand, and Erwin would come into the bedroom announcing, 'There's a bear in here. Where can it be?', looking in the corners, in the cupboard, behind the chair. If he didn't continue the search long enough, Sarah would encourage him. 'You haven't looked under the bed.' Finally he would say, 'There it is, in bed!' and she would shiver with excitement and say, 'Not me!'

'What did the Possum do that was very cheeky? What did it do that was terribly, terribly naughty?' It spilt milk all over the table, (something that Sarah was apt to do, to Erwin's annoyance). Or, it was eating bread and honey, and got honey all over the Bear. The Possum had to give the Bear a shower and wash its fur nicely and dry it, so that it was soft and clean again. Sarah stroked the air with her hands to show how soft and smooth the Bear had become, a tender gesture that she made on Erwin, on dogs and cats, even on her toys. 'She laughed so much at each outrageous instance of possum unruliness that it was hard to think of things cheeky enough.'

The cast of the stories grew. To Possum, Bear and Elephant were added a monkey, four horses, and Barby and Christy, two older girls with whom Sarah sometimes played. These creatures all lived together in a house at the beach with no grown-ups, and went for long walks, on which they sometimes encountered fierce animals. Erwin was seldom allowed to tell a story straightforwardly. Sarah would interrupt saying, 'No, it wasn't like that! Say it like this!' The Cheeky Possum met a crocodile, which was about to eat her. She called out for Barby and Christy, who came running, and hit the crocodile until it let go and ran away. 'No,' Sarah insisted, 'No, they didn't hit the crocodile. The crocodile suddenly got quite small, very, very small. It turned into a baby crocodile. It was all alone in the world, it had no mummy and daddy and no brother and no sister. So the Possum tucked it into her pram and took it home and looked after it.'

Sarah used to demand Cheeky Possum stories from me too, but mine were so pedestrian and repetitive that she soon got tired of them. Erwin expanded and embellished his for more than a year, until he too got bored, and took to reading a story at bedtime instead. But he painted a splendid panel for the playroom with all the animals on it, Sarah giving orders about what to include. In one corner, beneath the golden-furred possum, and the rose, tangerine, violet and blue horses, he drew at her request a scene from our first days at Portsea, Erwin, with Sarah riding on his shoulders, running from a snake in the sand dunes.

There was the same contrast between Erwin and me in daily conversation. My talk was earth-boundi; I explained, forewarned, recalled, reassured and consoled. His was airy and playful. There was, for example, a game of identities in which they took turns to ask questions. What are you? What colour are you? What do you eat? At first the replies were conventionally nonsensical. 'I'm large and round and black with blue stripes and I eat carrots and porridge.' But her questions began to hover around one theme: 'Do you eat children? Do you eat only very tiny children, or little children too? There's one here, do you eat children like this one?' And if Erwin made a grab for her, she would shriek with delight. When it was her turn to answer she said, 'I'm red and blue and green and I eat flowers.' 'Don't you eat people?' 'No, I don't hurt anyone. I only sniff people.'

Sarah had a work corner in Erwin's studio, with her own brushes and an old striped t-shirt of his, which she wore as an overall. 'I sometimes resented her interruptions when I was working, but I discovered that the easiest thing was to give her something to do. She never stayed long.'

A visitor to whom he was showing paintings asked her if she liked one of them. 'Of course! It's my Daddy's.'

He overheard her singing Baa Baa Black Sheep to Müttchen, who asked, 'What are you going to do with all that wool?' 'Make a pullover to keep my Daddy warm.'

'If I had something wrong, a cut finger, or a bad back, she would always ask, "Is your finger better, Daddy?" or "How is your back this morning?" She noticed what I wore. She said, "You've got your good suit on. You look very nice," and she would stroke it. She used to say, "I like you, Daddy. I like you very much. Do you like me?" It was straight lovers' talk, without any trace of anxiety, and very cheerful, because she knew the answer.'

Lying in the sun in the garden, he recalled, 'She would lie on me and say, "Oh such a nice cushion to lie on!" She loved me to roll her over and push her away. She would quietly roll back to my side, pretending to be asleep, so that I could push her away again. If I didn't do so straight away, she would say, "Again!" She often asked me at night, "Why don't you sleep in my bed?" and when I said, "There's not much room," she would reply, "I'll make room."'

I read out to Erwin a sentence from an authority on child psychology: 'Restrictions of the child's demands are taken as rebuff, the necessary refusal of bodily intimacy creates unhappiness, guilt and inhibition.' Applied to Sarah, this seemed to me (and still seems) absurd, but to my surprise he didn't immediately dismiss it. 'I don't know. I'd like to talk about it to Cecily. I spent a lot of time trying to detach myself gently from her on those nights when she most passionately wanted me to stay. I never reproved her, and there was always lots of kissing and cuddling, but I don't know.'

Another time, he said, 'Love and kissing were the

centre of her existence. She would say "Kiss! More kiss!" Already a long while ago she would say, "Kiss me on the forehead, kiss me on the cheek, kiss me on the ear," and so forth. At night, every night, she said, "I won't let you go, I'll never let you go." I didn't know what I should do. I tried to accept it lightly. She would hug me very close. But in the end she would say, "See you later, alligator." It was a sign of relaxing and meant that I could leave her.'

'Sometimes I used to feel so close to her that I knew what her reaction was going to be. I felt it in myself.'

'She used to say, "Wait for me!" It seemed to me an immensely touching appeal, which sums up the whole situation of the child. I couldn't possibly have disregarded it.'

Late Changes

After her fifth birthday, Sarah made another leap towards maturity. With the mingled awe and love we often felt as we watched her, Erwin and I noted an accumulation of incidents, trivial in themselves, but momentous because they were new for her. I recorded them later. What they hint at is elusive, belonging among those things which cannot be said clearly, like much that I have wanted to express about her life. They have to do with her growing self-confidence and awareness of being a separate person, with a will and a destiny of her own.

Not long before, she had gone for the first time alone to a strange house to have lunch with a schoolfriend. Erwin had taken her to school that morning, and reported that she hadn't wanted to be collected at the end of the morning by the other child's mother; but she had gone all the same; and when I fetched her, she was cheerfully proud of her courage.

A week later, she had set off confidently one Saturday morning to play at the house of another schoolfriend, and had brought home a bottle of 'perfume' made of bruised and browning flower petals steeped in water. That was a new kind of pastime also. Some childhood activities seem particularly fated to destroy illusion – those in which everyday raw materials are transformed, not just by imagination, but by mixing and moulding to form an object which seems real, until it starts disconcertingly to decay. I remember myself as a child making mud pies decorated with geranium petals, which looked entrancingly like little cakes with glistening chocolate icing, and my chagrin next day on finding that they had turned into lustreless clods of earth. I don't know whether Sarah experienced this disillusionment over her 'perfume', but the threat was there.

Perfume-making still had the imaginative freedom of a child's game. Other incidents, to do with her desire to share in adult activities, suggest that instead of simply indulging in the fantasy of being grown-up, she was becoming aware of what the situation required in reality.

Motel scene: Sarah sat properly at table during dinner, chose her meal, and asked when the 'server' was coming. Sarah talked to the server, and when she had eaten asked if she could go into the kitchen. We hesitated, but allowed her; I think she was usually welcome because she talked so easily and comprehensibly. When the waitress started to clear the tables, Sarah asked if she could help, and did help, taking exactly what she was told and putting it neatly on the girl's tray – the salts and peppers and plastic boxes for bread.

At home she wanted to help with household tasks, and between her perceptiveness and my reluctance to be held up, she was rarely a hindrance. She liked to give me the pegs when I was hanging up clothes, but since she couldn't keep up with me, I kept a supply to use in between. In the kitchen, she asked what she could do and accepted if I said there was nothing. She seldom undertook to try things by herself, though once, when I was mixing a cake, she picked up a spoon and tried to stir the bowl, but flipped a blob of batter onto the floor. She gave me a look of crestfallen guilt that stabbed me to the heart. When had I ever been so angry as to make her afraid? She didn't try again, but she greased the tin if I gave her a wad of paper and a pat of butter, making a good job of it.

When I weeded the herb bed, Daniel seized a couple of stems of parsley and some chives, and tugged, but Sarah waited until I showed her what was to be pulled out.

Six months ago, she used to help herself to make-up, and paint her face garishly and streakily. That time was past; she began to appreciate what was properly done. I had given her an old lipstick, worn down to the metal. She had picked it out as one I might spare and asked if she could have it. A few times she painted her lips very neatly, keeping to the natural outline.

Erwin: 'She helped me with the washing-up. I washed, and she put on her pink apron with the cat on it that Otti had given her, and dried the dishes very thoroughly and well. If she was trying to help but really being a nuisance, I used to say, "You're not really helping, you know," or "Look, you're only making a mess," and she would stop. She didn't like being told that what she was doing wasn't a real help.'

'When you were ill last month she quite changed her attitude, and there was less playing around. She was seriously concerned to be helpful. She hoovered the living-room really well. I plugged in the Hoover and she switched it on and did the whole room. It only needed touching up where she had tilted the Hoover because it was too big for her. She helped to get Daniel dressed, pointing out what clothes he wore, and how to tell the back from the front of his pants. She had an air of being in my confidence.'

All this was quite different from earlier play-acting, when she pretended to talk to Ossie Burt on the telephone, or to give Daniel a reading lesson. Indeed I wonder now, suddenly, whether it might have been her revolutionary discovery of what reading involved that made the difference – the discovery that it was useless just to imagine herself playing an adult role, that she must also look detachedly at what was there, outside herself.

Usually in the afternoon, after our reading lesson, I returned to my desk upstairs, while Sarah and Daniel went for a walk with Beverly. Sometimes, to escape from the cosiness of home, I went for a walk also, by myself, along the river, or through quiet streets that hadn't changed since my childhood. One damp afternoon, Sarah came into my room as I was about to leave. 'Where are you going?' she asked. 'I'm going for a walk.' 'Can I come with you?' I didn't want her. 'No, I'm going to walk very fast.' 'But I'll walk fast too. You won't have to wait for me.' I saw my hour of freedom slipping away, but her expression of yearning and vulnerability made refusal impossible. I helped her to put on her pale yellow raincoat, and tied an Indian silk scarf around her head. Sarah had liked its brilliant colours and pattern of tiny elephants, and asked if she could have it. It was part of a little hoard of possessions that she looked after carefully each time we moved.

We set off. I still felt cross, and strode rapidly down the hill past the tram depot. She trotted after me. We took one of my favourite walks, through an island of Victorian houses protected from the din of traffic by a loop of the river. She strained to keep up with me, her cheeks wet with drizzle. It began to rain more heavily, and she looked tired, but not until we were nearly home did she complain. Then she asked in a wavering voice, 'Is it much further?' and I softened, talked encouragingly to her, and took a short cut back home.

She had never before been so persistent in persuading me to do something I didn't want to do. Previously, she had accepted the patterns of presence and absence that Erwin and I had ordained. 'Make sure you say goodbye before you go to town,' she demanded, not aspiring to control more than the manner of my leaving. Her tears when we went out at night were a child's desperate way of relieving tension over what she is powerless to change. Even when she cried out, on being told that we were going out to dinner, 'Don't go! I don't want you to go,' it was from despair, not hope. But on the afternoon of our walk in the rain, she found a will strong enough to change the course of events.

One Sunday, soon afterwards, we were driving home along a street of untidy shops with iron-pillared verandahs, the Melbourne version of the indistinguishable streets which surround all big cities. We had still a long way to go, when Sarah announced, 'I was here with Beverly last week.' 'I don't think you can have been, darling,' I said. 'This is Brunswick. You can't have walked as far as this.' 'Yes, we did.' 'But we're miles from home. It must have been somewhere else that looked just like this.' 'No it wasn't. This is where we were.'

This was new too. She had always accepted without question any factual statement of mine. For a moment I wanted to insist that she acknowledge her mistake. Then I reflected that I could not give her a lesson in logic, since she understood too little about distances and suburban monotony. I could only bludgeon her into silence. Still feeling a bit miffed, I let the matter drop.

Unlike demands to be bought an ice cream, or her insistence on sharing my walk in the rain, her intransigence this time was an act of pure will. She had nothing to gain but victory itself. Her stubbornness reminds me that she was not simply a child living in acceptance of parental love and authority, but a human being, separate, unique, striving erratically towards autonomy.

Talk

'Listen to me! I want to *tell* you something!' I see her racing across the garden, hair flapping, to confront me, or anyone, with a long, impetuous account of what had just happened.

Sarah was an accomplished and voluble talker. But

spoken words are heard once and then lost forever. Almost always. Fragments of children's conversation recorded by others sometimes bring Sarah vividly before me, but her own words have vanished. Except for those recorded in my first notes about her, when I set down every saying of hers that I could remember, however fragmentary. There is not much that could be called conversation, none of her long excited narratives, and only scraps of the commentary that often accompanied whatever she was doing. But there are isolated words and phrases that she used repeatedly, appearing to relish them as much for their sound, or their place in a recurring situation, as for their meaning. Language was a game or a ritual as well as a means of communication.

'What's your name?' Questioned by a stranger, she would reply, 'Sarah Janey Why Fabian, because I talk so much.' 'Why' had been added by Betty, with a faint air of disapproval, since too much talk wasn't really liked. But Sarah was proud of the addition and relished having a long name to reel off. She knew and liked to recite the full names of each member of the family. 'Where do you go to school?' 'The Robin Cochrane Free Kindergarten.' She always gave the full title, though substituting 'Robin' for 'Robert'.

Sarah asked questions in return: What's your name? Have you got any children? Have you got a dog or a cat? Are you married? Questions not asked pertly, but out of concern that the stranger should not live alone. In a guest house in Portland, she introduced us to a middle-aged woman. 'This is Jessie. She's got a cat called Peter. She's a teacher.' Next morning, when we were preparing to leave, she ran off, explaining, 'I must say goodbye to Jessie.'

In a mountain picnic ground, we stopped to make tea on a crisp winter morning, because a large can of water simmered invitingly on a glowing fire, there for all comers. We went to speak to two elderly ladies, so that Sarah could pat their dog. They came from Mitcham, one of them said. 'My nurse lives in Mitcham," Sarah replied. 'She's going to be married and I'm going to the wedding. I'm going to be allowed into the church if I behave myself.' The ladies looked taken aback by this revelation. 'Well you'd better behave yourself,' said one, with a laugh.

'I'm going to investigate!' she proclaimed, hopping out of the car at a petrol station in the country. For once I could identify the source of one of her phrases – Turkey, in *The Little Red Hen*.

'I'm escaping like mad!' she would announce to me as she slipped out of my hands at bedtime. To Erwin, in the course of some loving mistreatment, 'I'm clambering eagerly on you!' She loved adverbs, and often used them to start a sentence: 'Actually. . . ', 'Presumably. . . ', 'Luckily. . .'

'I'll be a bit shy at first,' she said, if we were going to visit people she didn't know. But I don't remember that she ever was.

As new parents, we had looked forward rather dubiously to being called Mummy and Daddy, and hadn't encouraged her to use these terms. She adopted them nevertheless, of course, spoken with such pride that we were won over. Sometimes she called me 'Mother', tentatively, experimenting to see how she liked it, watching me to see how I received it. Very rarely she called me 'Pat', with a look that acknowledged her daring.

If we wanted to conceal something from her, we spoke French, referring to her as 'la petite'. She understood our motive and recognised her code-name but didn't seem resentful. 'La petite, n'est ce pas?' she would say, getting in on the act. She pronounced the occasional French word beautifully, copying Erwin, who had been to a French lycée, and retained an impeccable accent though not much else. I resolved to buy her a French story-book, since I thought that to cultivate such a talent would be a pleasure for both of us. When Müttchen spoke German, her response was a slightly patronising parody: 'Müttchen, cav, div, div, div.'

Until she was about five, she never asked me the meaning of any word in the stories I read to her, although they must have been a fertile source of her expanding vocabulary. Then she began to pick out an occasional word and ask me what it meant. After that, if we re-read the story, she would stop at the same place to ask the meaning of the same word, not enquiringly but in a chanting tone, and without listening to the answer, changing a request for information into a ritual, as if the conquest of language like physical growth ought to unfold without conscious effort.

Out shopping, if another car slid ahead of us into a parking space, she would call out triumphantly, 'They just snitched it!' relishing both the phrase and the contest, taking sides against us. 'Does it say no parking at any time?' she asked repeatedly, adding another formula to the ritual of daily life, savouring the fact that the adult world also contained prohibitions.

Mealtimes produced a crop of sayings. 'Soup! My

favourite!', 'Fish, fish, my favourite dish!', 'I'm a cheese-eater!' (from hearing Betty say to Erwin, 'I know you're not a potato-eater, so I've given you plenty of cauliflower.') 'Offer me! Offer me!'– a demand that a dish be presented to her so that she could help herself, like a guest. To Müttchen, whom she liked to bully a little, 'You mustn't eat that, it's just for decoration.' Sometimes, with disarming frankness, when offered a piece of cake, 'Which is the biggest?'

'Not sweet enough!' she proclaimed regularly when we sugared her drink or her cereal, a tease based on the knowledge that we didn't want her to take too much sugar. There were a number of such chants, which could be repeated indefinitely, Daniel joining in. 'Yoomy goomy yoomy goomy. . .' when anything she particularly liked was served.

Other chants were kept up interminably on long drives, to release pent-up energy and punish the imprisoning parents. 'Faster, faster, faster', they would urge as we negotiated a narrow mountain road. 'How many miles?' she would demand in a strident voice, leaning over the back of the seat, when we passed a milepost, especially if we planned to stay away for the night. The answer meant nothing to her, it was a ritual to break up those endless tracts of unfamiliar territory. 'Are we going to stay in a hotel-motel, or just a motel?' was simply word-tasting.

She brought a riddle home from nursery school: 'If an elephant sat on a fence, what time would it be? Say "I don't know."' 'I don't know.' Sarah, 'Time to get a new fence!' This exchange was repeated many times, Sarah's pleasure not diminishing with repetition or lack of surprise. Nor did she introduce variations, as Daniel did when eventually he learned the same riddle at the same school. 'If an elephant sat on a cake. . . ', or, 'Time to get a new elephant.'

School also taught her obscenities ('Poo in your whiskers!') and the worst words she knew ('Shit, bugger, idiot, poo!') a list chanted defiantly in unison with Daniel.

'You're not my friend!' This was the most hostile of her sayings, and even then she was usually half joking. On a very few occasions, when she was upset and crying, she said, 'Go away, I don't want you.' Never, to anyone, 'I hate you!' Erwin and I agreed emphatically on this.

She recited the grace she had learned at nursery school:

Thank you for the food we eat;
Thank you for the world so sweet;
Thank you for the birds that sing;
Thank you, God, for everything.

And she would continue, improvising, 'Thank you for the flowers, thank you for the sun, thank you for the trees, thank you for the cats.' But not 'Thank you for Mummy and Daddy and Daniel', who were too much part of her own self to be thought of as gifts.

And there was another chant: 'Yes, no, yes, no, yes, no. . .' A reply to a question, any question, perhaps something as simple as whether she wanted more milk. She intoned it in a loud emphatic sing-song, with a look of gleeful stubbornness, as if she might go on for ever, relishing her power to keep us waiting, and ridiculing the very idea of choice. Accepting all the alternatives, accepting everything.

Acknowledgements

Author and Editor gratefully acknowledge the following:

Carcanet Press Limited for permission to reprint lines from 'Sick Love', by Robert Graves, *Complete Poems in One Volume*.

Klaus Friedeberger for permission to reproduce Photographs 1-5.

Photographs 6 and 7 are by Erwin Fabian.

Photograph 8 is by Hugo Wolfsohn.